"Leland Ryken is a master anthologist with an encyclopedic knowledge of devotional poetry and literature. This Yuletide anthology is a rich feast designed to nourish the soul on the truth and wonder of the incarnation with a masterful selection of hymns, devotionals, and poems."

Gregory E. Reynolds, Editor, *Ordained Servant*; author, *The Word Is Worth a Thousand Pictures* and *Yuletide: Poems and Artwork*

"Leland Ryken's *Journey to Bethlehem* is such a rich resource. Sometimes it's overwhelming how many books, devotionals, and resources exist for Advent. Ryken solves the problem by curating the best of the best for us. This volume will become an annual coffee-table staple in our household!"

Brett McCracken, Senior Editor, The Gospel Coalition; author, *The Wisdom Pyramid*

"What a valuable collection of Christmas gems: classic hymns, devotionals, and poems that celebrate Christ's coming with words of weight and beauty. They are polished and packaged for us here, offered with just enough background and explication to help us relish and understand. This is a Christmas gift that will last."

Kathleen Nielson, author; speaker

"This powerful but accessible volume instructs, delights, and edifies. It is a blessing that readers will long to share with others."

David V. Urban, Professor of English, Calvin University; author, *Milton and the Parables of Jesus*

"Leland Ryken has been rendering great service to the church by recovering its rich devotional heritage and making it accessible for contemporary Christians. Now he takes up Christmas, the favorite holiday, helping us meditate on the birth of Christ by unpacking the classic works of songwriters, poets, and theologians."

Gene Edward Veith Jr., Professor of Literature Emeritus, Patrick Henry College; author, *Reading Between the Lines: A Christian Guide to Literature*

"This volume provides the reader with a rich selection of well-edited Christmas texts drawn from across the ages, selected for their unique perspectives and artistic expression, and paired with thoughtful essays. The texts and commentaries are brief enough to read as devotionals, say after a family meal, and weighty enough to prompt one to ponder throughout the day."

James C. Wilhoit, Professor of Christian Education Emeritus, Wheaton College

"Advent can often feel like a treasure barely opened; we can tell the glories go far deeper than we've seen, even after many seasons. In *Journey to Bethlehem*, Leland Ryken plunders the poems and prose of Christian history to help us pause before the manger and, with the shepherds, stand in deeper awe. The devotionals included here shed fresh light at every turn, showing the riches of Christ more clearly—and showing why those riches are called 'unsearchable.'"

Scott Hubbard, Editor, Desiring God; Lay Pastor, All Peoples Church, Minneapolis, Minnesota

JOURNEY TO BETHLEHEM

JOURNEY TO BETHLEHEM

A Treasury of Classic Christmas Devotionals

Leland Ryken, editor

CROSSWAY®

WHEATON, ILLINOIS

Library of Congress Cataloging-in-Publication Data

Names: Ryken, Leland, editor.
Title: Journey to Bethlehem : a treasury of classic Christmas devotionals / Leland Ryken, editor.
Description: Wheaton, Illinois : Crossway, 2023. | Includes bibliographical references and index.
Identifiers: LCCN 2022032559 (print) | LCCN 2022032560 (ebook) | ISBN 9781433584190 (cloth) | ISBN 9781433584206 (pdf) | ISBN 9781433584220 (epub)
Subjects: LCSH: Christmas—Literary collections. | Christmas stories. | Christmas poetry. | Hymns.
Classification: LCC PN6071.C6 J68 2023 (print) | LCC PN6071.C6 (ebook) | DDC 808.8/0334—dc23/eng/20220927
LC record available at https://lccn.loc.gov/2022032559
LC ebook record available at https://lccn.loc.gov/2022032560

Crossway is a publishing ministry of Good News Publishers.

RRDS		32	31	30	29	28	27	26	25	24	23
15	14	13	12	11	10	9	8	7	6	5	4	3	2	1

For Tom and Dyanne Martin

Contents

Editor's Introduction

This book is an anthology of classic Christmas devotionals. As I did the research for this book, it quickly became obvious that the Christian world needs an alternative to the lightweight Christmas books that flood the market. The classic texts that I have brought together in this volume have stood the test of time and for discernible reasons.

The word *classic* in this book's title is not simply honorific but denotes specific qualities of the texts that make up this anthology. One of these traits is that the authors and/or texts are famous. I hope that as my readers read the table of contents, they will have their curiosity aroused by questions such as: *What did Luther, Calvin, Spurgeon, and other famous preachers say in their Christmas sermons? Why are hymns included as examples of devotional poems? What ten Christmas poems rose to the top in the field?* In regard to the last question, I will share a secret: as I envisioned my project of collecting classic Christmas literature, I assumed that the section of poems would be the easiest to fill, but in fact it was difficult to find ten Christmas poems that were sufficiently weighty to lend themselves to a five-hundred-word analysis.

Being famous is one criterion for being a classic, but what qualities make a devotional famous? The answers fall into the categories of *content* and *form*. At the level of content, a devotional included in this anthology needs to yield fresh insight into Christmas. Often there is a surprise twist or paradoxical aspect to a classic devotional. We are left feeling that we have never thought of the situation in that particular way before. Because of this original slant, a classic devotional stays in our memories or at least strikes us as being worthy of being a permanent part of our experience even on a first reading. The Bible speaks of singing a new song, and the devotionals in this anthology are either literally or figuratively a new song of Christmas. A classic devotional gives us more than we already know.

If we turn to the *form* and *style* of a classic devotional, the quality of originality just noted applies here too. Excellence of style consists partly in the freshness of expression. Literary qualities also elevate a passage above conventional expository discourse. The presence of figurative language is a prevalent but not indispensable technique. Verbal beauty, or what we call a well-turned phrase, is equally characteristic of the selections in this book. Readers of the devotionals in this anthology will feel artistically as well as spiritually refreshed.

These qualities of content and form relate to the explications that accompany the selections in this book. *Explication* is the term that literary scholars use for the practice of close reading of a text. The close readings of the passages in this book were governed by the impulse to show what makes each passage great at the levels of both spiritual edification and excellence of expression.

Several principles determined the selection of devotional texts for this anthology. The first criterion was spiritual edification. The second was that the selections as a group met the test of being the best in their categories. Because they all meet that criterion, they are also a roll call of the famous. In this regard, there is a latent educational agenda at work. In the history of theology, why is the name of Athanasius automatically linked with the incarnation? Why, according to a survey, is "Silent Night" the world's most popular Christmas hymn ever? What was the very first Christmas poem? Why does the Nicene Creed replace the Apostles' Creed in Sunday morning services during December in some churches? For people who have a curiosity about these and similar matters, this book will provide answers.

I hope that my readers will not be disappointed by my refusal to say anything in this introduction about the history of Christmas as an observance. It is not relevant to the subject of this book. Although all of the selections in this anthology were *occasioned by* the celebration of Christmas, they are not *about* the institution that we know as Christmas. They are about the events of the nativity and incarnation as recorded in the Bible, along with the meaning of those events.

Some readers will have noticed by now that I have not used the word *advent* in connection with this anthology. Is this an advent book? Yes and no. If we define the word *advent* to mean "coming or arrival," it is an advent book, concerned from start to finish with the coming of Jesus to earth in human form. Similarly, if we think of advent in a liturgical sense of preparing for the coming of Christmas, the definition again fits, and in fact the thirty selections could be read during the weeks of December ending on Christmas Eve. But at the level of content or subject matter, the selections do not deal with preparation for Christ's coming to earth. They are instead about the events of the nativity and incarnation as accomplished facts.

I also need to make a distinction between the genres of anthology and a book of daily readings in a devotional book based on the calendar. An anthology is not tied to a schedule. It can be read in a week if one desires. It can be dipped into intermittently, with no guilt feelings about having missed a day. Of course the determination of thirty selections invites daily reading according to the traditional Advent period of late November through December 24. But even here there is a twist: one is unlikely to reread a calendar devotional book after the days have passed, whereas I hope that the readers of this anthology will reread it many times and do so year round.

Everything that I have said in this introduction is a variation on a central theme, namely, that this anthology provides something new. The mixture of the three categories of hymns-as-poems, prose selections, and poems is new. Limiting the selections to famous classic texts is new. Accompanying each passage with a five-hundred-word analysis is new.

All of the entries in this anthology follow an identical format: (1) the devotional text; (2) an analysis and explication of the text; (3) a summing up paragraph that identifies the practical takeaway of the entry; (4) a parallel Bible passage that clinches and enhances the devotional experience. All of this will seem familiar to some of my readers because this anthology is a companion to two previous Crossway books—*The Soul in Paraphrase: A Treasury of Classic Devotional Poems* and *The Heart in Pilgrimage: A Treasury of Classic Devotionals on the Christian Life.*

The best way to combine the devotional passages with the explications is first to read the devotional entry, then read the explication as a way of reaching a fuller understanding and enjoyment of what you have just read, and then read the devotional a second time, using the tips from the explication as a lens through which to view the passage more fully.

PART 1

CHRISTMAS HYMNS

Every hymn begins its life as a poem. It becomes a hymn only when it is paired with music. Until the 1870s, hymnbooks were words-only books, five inches by three inches in size. They were essentially anthologies of devotional poems. Our experience of hymns is revolutionized when we see them printed as poems and interact with them as devotional poems.

The first thing we see is that the text was composed on the principle of the line as the basic and recurrent unit of thought. The sentences do not run all the way to the right margin. If hymnic poems are composed on the principle of line construction, we need to read them that way. When we do, we immediately sense that the thought units are much briefer and more succinct than prose is.

A second thing we note is that the flow of thought in a hymnic poem is packaged as a series of stanzas. We do not fully experience this until we see the stanzas before us in vertical sequence. The progression is not circular, as when we return to the same starting point in a hymnbook but sequential. Then as we stare at the stanzas arranged in this way, we can identify the specific function of each stanza in the ongoing flow and in the overall superstructure.

When these things are in view, we can take the next step to identify the unifying theme or "big idea" of the poem. Usually a poet signals the unifying idea or motif of a poem in the first line or two. Once we train ourselves to identify the unifying core of a hymnic poem, we naturally start to think in terms of theme and variation (a formula borrowed from music). The individual stanzas are not self-contained units but are building blocks in a coherent whole.

The foregoing considerations have to do with the organization or structure of a poem. We need to balance that with the poetic texture—the individual details such as images and figures of speech. It takes time to unpack the meanings of these details, and treating a hymn as a poem allows us take the time that is required, instead of being forced to resort to the speed reading that singing necessarily imposes.

The explications in this section include material that has been re-purposed from my book *40 Favorite Hymns of the Christian Year* (2020), published by Presbyterian and Reformed Publishing Company; acknowledgment is hereby gratefully recorded (see acknowledgments page for more information).

1

Joy to the World

ISAAC WATTS (1674–1748)

Joy to the world! the Lord is come;
Let earth receive her King;
Let every heart prepare him room,
And heaven and nature sing.

Joy to the earth! the Savior reigns;
Let men their songs employ;
While fields and floods, rocks, hills, and plains
Repeat the sounding joy.

No more let sins and sorrows grow,
Nor thorns infest the ground;
He comes to make his blessings flow
Far as the curse is found.

He rules the world with truth and grace,
And makes the nations prove
The glories of his righteousness,
And wonders of his love.

It is natural to begin the section of Christmas hymns with the hymn often chosen to begin a congregational Christmas service. It is doubly appropriate to begin with it because the author is none other than the person known to posterity as "the father of English hymnody." Isaac Watts (1674–1748), an educator and author of books on wide-ranging subjects, is regarded as a fountainhead figure in the history of hymnody because he is the one who freed hymn singing from the single-minded adherence to Psalm paraphrases (also known as metrical psalms). Watts wrote some 750 hymns.

The most obvious quality of "Joy to the World" is the tone of exuberance that breathes through it from start to finish. The opening word gets the excitement started with the accented word *Joy*, and after that everything is part of a grand celebration.

The opening line states the unifying idea of the poem, namely, the coming of Christ to earth in the incarnation and the joy that accompanies that coming. Everything that follows is an elaboration of this opening sentence. A discernible division of duties is present between the first two stanzas and the final two.

The first two stanzas focus on the coming itself. These stanzas are filled with references to the nativity story, with the imagery of coming, the angels' pronouncement of *joy* that resounded over the countryside, mention of the *fields* where the shepherds were abiding with their sheep, reference to four nativity *songs* recorded in Luke's Gospel, the joining of *heaven and nature* in the angels' poetic words to the shepherds, and the need to *prepare room* for Jesus (an implied rebuke of how at Jesus's birth there was no room in the inn). In our imaginations we journey to Bethlehem on the night of Jesus's birth.

We can hardly miss the element of command in the first two stanzas, as expressed in the imperative verb *let*. The command to praise is a standard feature in the praise psalms of the Old Testament, and its presence here alerts us that this is a poem of praise. After the praise psalms state a command to praise and name the recipients of the command (as stanzas 1–2 of this hymn do as well), they outline the reason why we should offer praise. That is exactly what the final two stanzas of "Joy to the World" do.

These stanzas shift our attention from the coming of Jesus to earth to the effects of his coming. We continue to participate in a grand celebration in these stanzas, which are a partly literal and partly figurative picture of the blessings of the messianic reign that began when Christ came to earth to accomplish his great work of redemption. Stanza 3 asserts that the coming of Jesus has reversed the effects of the fall, as pronounced by God in the curse of Genesis 3:17–18. The last stanza balances this act of cancelation of what is *no more* with a positive picture of what Christ has brought with his universal spiritual rule, with emphasis on *righteousness* and *love*. The exuberance continues unabated here at the end with the words *glories* and *wonders*.[1]

The devotional takeaway from this poem follows the contour of the poem itself: we should celebrate Christmas with the joy that the hymn commands, and we should secure our position as recipients of the blessings of Christ's messianic rule as delineated in the two concluding stanzas.

This hymnic poem arose from Isaac Watts's famous enterprise of giving the Old Testament Psalms a Christological interpretation. Psalm 96:10–13 is a particularly close parallel to "Joy to the World":

> Say among the nations, "The LORD reigns! . . .
> Let the heavens be glad, and let the earth rejoice;
>   let the sea roar, and all that fills it;
>   let the field exult, and everything in it!
> Then shall all the trees of the forest sing for joy
>   before the LORD, for he comes. . . .

2

Angels from the Realms of Glory

JAMES MONTGOMERY (1771–1854)

Angels from the realms of glory,
Wing your flight o'er all the earth;
Ye who sang creation's story,
Now proclaim Messiah's birth.

Shepherds in the fields abiding,
Watching o'er your flocks by night,
God with man is now residing,
Yonder shines the infant light.

Sages, leave your contemplations,
Brighter visions beam afar;
Seek the great Desire of nations;
Ye have seen his natal star.

Saints before the altar bending,
Watching long in hope and fear,
Suddenly the Lord, descending,
In his temple shall appear.

All creation, join in praising
God the Father, Spirit, Son;
Evermore your voices raising
To the eternal Three in One.

Refrain
Come and worship, come and worship,
Worship Christ, the newborn King.

Orphaned at age twelve and a dropout from grade school shortly there-after, Scottish-born James Montgomery (1771–1854) would seem to be an unlikely candidate to write four hundred hymns, including "Prayer Is the Soul's Sincere Desire." Shortly before Christmas of 1816, Montgomery, then age forty-five, read the Christmas story from Luke 2. The song of the angels seized his imagination, and the words of a poem took shape. As is true of many hymns, inspiration caused the words to flow, and Montgomery completed the poem by day's end. He printed it a day later, on Christmas Eve, in the local newspaper that he owned.

Most hymnic poems signal in the opening line what the controlling theme of the entire poem will be, but in this instance that expectation is misleading. The poem is not only about the angels of the nativity but also presents a pageant of nearly all the major agents in the Christmas story. In successive stanzas, we are led to contemplate the *angels*, the *shepherds*, the wise men (*sages*), Simeon and Anna (*saints*), and finally *all creation*.

Then as we look more closely, we begin to see what a packed and subtle poem this is. The poetic strategy of addressing someone absent as though present and capable of responding is called *apostrophe*. That is what this poem employs in every stanza as well as the refrain. The understood rule is that apostrophe is a way of expressing strong feel-ing, and if we note further that the speaker in the poem is busy issuing commands from start to finish, we can scarcely avoid being swept up into the rhapsody that is unfolding before us.

As we look still more closely, we see that in the first four stanzas the agents who are successively addressed are commanded to leave their customary activity and turn instead to the newly born Jesus. For example, the angels reside in heaven, and they sang at the creation of the world (Job 38:7), but now they are commanded to wing their flight to Bethlehem. It is likewise with the shepherds who ordinarily watch their flocks, the wise men who contemplate the stars, and Simeon and Anna who worship in anticipation in the temple. The final stanza breaks the pattern by introducing a liturgical ingredient that sounds the perfect note of closure.

Nothing more would seem to be possible in this procession, but something more *is* possible. The refrain, actually a doxology (a command to praise God), brings *us* into the drama, as we are commanded and invited to do what the angels, shepherds, wise men, and Simeon and Anna did. And all that we have noted is expressed with an eloquence and verbal beauty that are breathtaking.[2]

As we leave this beautiful devotional poem, we should allow ourselves to agree with the poet that leaving our ordinary concerns behind for the moment and journeying to Bethlehem instead are the order of the day. Worshiping the newborn King is what the Christmas season calls us to.

The following is the text that prompted Montgomery's inspired response:

And suddenly there was with the angel a multitude of the heavenly host praising God and saying,

"Glory to God in the highest,
    and on earth peace among those with whom he is
    pleased!" (Luke 2:13–14)

3

Come, Thou Long-Expected Jesus

CHARLES WESLEY (1707–1788)

Come, thou long-expected Jesus,
Born to set thy people free;
From our fears and sins release us;
Let us find our rest in thee.

Israel's strength and consolation,
Hope of all the earth thou art;
Dear Desire of every nation,
Joy of every longing heart.

Born thy people to deliver,
Born a child, and yet a King,
Born to reign in us for ever,
Now thy gracious kingdom bring.

By thine own eternal Spirit
Rule in all our hearts alone;
By thine all-sufficient merit
Raise us to thy glorious throne.

This hymn was written by the most prolific English hymn writer of all time. Charles Wesley (1707–1788), brother of the evangelist John Wesley, wrote approximately 6,500 hymns, placing Wesley second only to American hymn-writer Fanny Crosby. "Come, Thou Long-Expected Jesus" was written in 1744 but was mainly only known in Methodist circles for a century. Then in 1855 a twenty-one-year-old Baptist minister in London named Charles Spurgeon quoted from it in his Christmas sermon, and after that it became a standard Christmas hymn in all Protestant denominations.

The first thing we notice is the pleasing simplicity of the poem. The stanzas are short and fall into the simplest stanzaic form in English poetry. It is called the *quatrain*, with alternate lines rhyming in an *abab* pattern. The entire poem, moreover, is a prayer addressed to Jesus by believers as a group (*our*, *us*). This simplicity of form is played off against the exaltation and eloquence of the words and phrases.

Once we move beyond the simplicity of the poem's form, the poem requires our best analytic powers, lest we misinterpret it. First, despite the fact that the word *born* appears four times, this poem is not about the nativity as an event. It is about the incarnation as a theological fact. The poem is nothing less than an exposition of what the coming of Jesus in human form accomplished for those who believe in him as Savior.

It is particularly important that we get the opening line right. It does not ask us to perform an act of imagination and become an Old Testament believer looking to a coming Messiah. The poem situates us in our own present experience. The opening petition *Come* is the first of six petitions in the poem. It does not invite Jesus to be born in Bethlehem but instead invites him to apply his already accomplished acts of redemption in our own lives. The phrase *thou long-expected Jesus* is a stately epithet or title for Jesus that calls attention to the fact that he was foretold and longed for throughout Old Testament history.

Each quatrain performs its own function in the unfolding design. The first stanza asks Jesus to free and release us from our sin. The second stanza momentarily drops the petitionary mode and is an outpouring of adoration to Jesus as the *strength, consolation, hope, desire*, and *joy* of *every nation* and *every longing heart*. Stanza 3 devotes three lines to rehearsing why Jesus was born, and then the last line petitions Jesus to bring his eternal kingdom. The last stanza is wholly petitionary, as two parallel pairs of lines, beginning with the formula "*by thine* _____," ask Jesus to rule in our hearts and raise us to heaven.[3]

The purpose of the poem is to define who Jesus is and what he came to earth to accomplish. We can absorb the poem best by allowing it to codify our understanding of the incarnation and by allowing the statements of longing and adoration to express our own feelings.

This hymnic poem is a meditation on why Jesus came to earth in the flesh. Zechariah's song recorded in Luke 1 does the same:

> Blessed be the Lord God of Israel,
>   for he has visited and redeemed his people
> and has raised up a horn of salvation for us . . .
>   (vv. 68–69)

4

Brightest and Best of the Sons of the Morning

REGINALD HEBER (1783–1826)

Brightest and best of the sons of the morning,
Dawn on our darkness, and lend us thine aid;
Star of the East, the horizon adorning,
Guide where our infant Redeemer is laid.

Cold on his cradle the dewdrops are shining;
Low lies his head with the beasts of the stall;
Angels adore him in slumber reclining,
Maker and Monarch, and Lord over all.

Say, shall we yield him, in costly devotion,
Odors of Edom, and offerings divine,
Gems of the mountain and pearls of the ocean,
Myrrh from the forest or gold from the mine?

Vainly we offer each ample oblation,
Vainly with gifts would his favor secure;
Richer by far is the heart's adoration;
Dearer to God are the prayers of the poor.

When poets sit down to compose Christmas hymns, they first choose a specific event or group of characters from the nativity story as the focus of their poems. As they work with the selected material, they do two things. First they imagine the details of the actual event and characters, making them come alive in our imaginations and enabling us to be vicariously present at the first Christmas. Then they subject the situation to meditative analysis and draw an application for us. The vehicle for this application is that the events and characters are viewed as *examples* of universal principles that apply to us. "Brightest and Best of the Sons of the Morning" does all these things, though it adds a surprise ending that breaks the pattern.

The event that Reginald Heber (1783–1826), an Anglican clergyman, chose for meditation in his poem is the journey of the wise men. Matthew's story of the journey of the wise men and their worship of the infant Jesus provides the entire frame of reference for this poem. Within this unifying framework, each stanza plays a part in the unfolding meditation, with the material arranged into pairs of stanzas, yielding a two-part structure overall.

The first stanza focuses on the star that led the wise men. The opening line introduces the note of eloquence that characterizes this literary hymn with a majestic epithet, or title, for the eastern star: *brightest and best of the sons of the morning*. The whole opening stanza is placed in the mouths of the wise men, as they petition the star to guide them on their journey. The second stanza then pictures what the wise men find when they arrive at the manger. The technique is not realistic but idealized with the intended purpose of expressing adoration. We should also note that in this stanza the first three lines picture the infant Jesus, and then the last line introduces a contrast by soaring with the divinity of the Christ child, who is declared to be *Maker and Monarch, and Lord over all*.

After the first two stanzas have taken our imaginations to the journey of the wise men, the second half of the poem raises a question of momentous spiritual importance, namely, What constitutes an adequate gift to bring the Christ child? The third stanza raises the possibility that the best gift is costly perfumes and jewels, in keeping with what the wise men are recorded as offering to Jesus in Matthew's Gospel. Our inclination is to agree with the suggestion that Jesus deserves costly gifts.

Then, in a surprise ending, the first two lines of the final stanza rebuke us for thinking that costly gifts are best. They are *vainly* offered, as *the heart's adoration* and *prayers of the poor* are said to be, paradoxically, *richer by far* and *dearer*.[4]

The last two lines of this hymn provide the application for this devotional. We cannot literally do what the wise men did, and we should not try. Adoring Christ in our hearts with the modest means we possess is our best gift.

This hymnic poem makes creative use of the journey and adoration of the magi. Here is the biblical subtext on which the poem is constructed:

And behold, the star that they had seen when it rose went before them until it came to rest over the place where the child was. When they saw the star, they rejoiced exceedingly with great joy. . . . and they fell down and worshiped him [and] offered him gifts, gold and frankincense and myrrh. (Matt. 2:9–11)

5

It Came upon the Midnight Clear

EDMUND SEARS (1810–1876)

It came upon the midnight clear,
That glorious song of old,
From angels bending near the earth,
To touch their harps of gold:
"Peace on the earth, goodwill to men,
From heaven's all-gracious King."
The world in solemn stillness lay,
To hear the angels sing.

Still through the cloven skies they
        come,
With peaceful wings unfurled,
And still their heavenly music floats
O'er all the weary world;
Above its sad and lowly plains,
They bend on hovering wing,
And ever o'er its babel sounds
The blessed angels sing.

Yet with the woes of sin and strife
The world has suffered long;
Beneath the angel-strain have rolled
Two thousand years of wrong;
And man, at war with man, hears not
The love-song which they bring;
O hush the noise, ye men of strife,
And hear the angels sing.

And ye, beneath life's crushing load,
Whose forms are bending low,
Who toil along the climbing way
With painful steps and slow,
Look now! for glad and golden hours
come swiftly on the wing.
O rest beside the weary road,
And hear the angels sing!

For lo! the days are hastening on,
By prophet bards foretold,
When with the ever-circling years
Comes round the age of gold,
When peace shall over all the earth
Its ancient splendors fling,
And the whole world give back the song
Which now the angels sing.

———

This weighty hymnic poem was written, as many hymns have been, by a cleric. It follows the nearly inevitable paradigm of a Christmas hymn. The starting point is Edmund Sears's (1810–1876) selection of a specific event and cast of characters from the nativity story. In this instance he chose the angels and their song, as highlighted in the last line of every stanza. Having led us to relive that part of the nativity story, the poem becomes meditative, in effect subjecting the event to analysis. The middle three stanzas of this hymn illustrate how this works. What we call a meditative poem has a strong element of application, so we should be looking for the poet's hints regarding how we can apply the story of the angels' song. Finally, Christmas poems do not simply end but are rounded off with a note of closure that influences the spirit in which we leave the poem.

The opening stanza of this poem offers the good news that we expect in a Christmas poem. We read about the atmospheric beauty of the *midnight clear*, the welcome visitation of the angels *bending near the earth*, and the comforting content of the angels' song of *peace* and *goodwill*. It is a variation on the theme that all is right in the world.

But then the poet springs a surprise on us. Instead of continuing the "feel good" mood of the opening stanza, a contest emerges between the voices of pessimism and optimism. Stanza 2 eases us in this direction by being a transition: it assures us that the angels' song is still available to us, but the world to which that song comes is said to be *weary* and *sad*. Following that, stanzas 3 and 4 are built around an extended conflict. The optimistic picture of *peace* and *goodwill* pronounced by the angels is pitted against a realistic picture of continuing *strife* among nations and misery in people's personal lives. The final stanza resolves the conflict with a prophecy of a coming golden age of universal peace, best interpreted as a picture of the heavenly world to come.

To recap, the five stanzas present the following variations on the chosen subject: the angels' song (1) as originally delivered, (2) declared to be still offered to the world, (3) ignored by a sinful world, (4) offered personally to suffering humanity, and (5) predicted to be perfectly realized in the coming eschaton.[5]

As we leave our encounter with this hymnic poem, we can heed its message of realism. The goodwill pronounced by the angels should not be the occasion for glibness, but rather received as good news for those who meet the requirements that make it possible. We should ponder what the angels' message means in a fallen world.

This poem is a meditation on the message of the angels, which the Gospel of Luke records in this way:

> And suddenly there was with the angel a multitude of the heavenly host praising God, and saying, Glory to God in the highest, and on earth peace, good will toward men. (Luke 2:13–14 KJV)

6

Once in Royal David's City

CECIL FRANCES ALEXANDER (1818–1895)

Once in royal David's city
Stood a lowly cattle shed,
Where a mother laid her baby
In a manger for his bed:
Mary was that mother mild,
Jesus Christ her little child.

He came down to earth from heaven
Who is God and Lord of all,
And his shelter was a stable,
And his cradle was a stall:
With the poor, and meek, and lowly,
Lived on earth our Savior holy.

And our eyes at last shall see him,
Through his own redeeming love;
For that Child so dear and gentle
Is our Lord in heaven above,
And he leads his children on
To the place where he is gone.

Not in that poor lowly stable,
With the oxen standing by,
We shall see him, but in heaven,
Set at God's right hand on high;
When like stars his children crowned
All in white shall wait around.

———

This hymn began its life as a poem for children, and not with Christmas specifically in view. Its author, Cecil Frances Alexander (1818–1895), wife of an Irish bishop, wrote a collection of poems designed to teach parts of the Apostles' Creed to children. "Once in Royal David's City" was linked to the statement in the Creed that Christ "was born of the virgin Mary," though it is just as strongly linked to the later statement, "He ascended into heaven and sits on the right hand of God the Father almighty."

The poem is built on the principle of contrast. The first two stanzas tell the story of Christ's nativity and are set in the most humble of earthly circumstances. The final two stanzas are set in heaven. The nativity stanzas tie into the theological concept of Christ's humiliation, and the last two stanzas express the theological concept of Christ's exaltation. The first movement portrays Christ's coming down from heaven to earth, and the second movement pictures our rising from earth to heaven. The first half looks backward in time, and the second half looks to the future life. Upon further analysis, we come to see that the second half of the poem gives us the reason for Christ's coming down, namely, bringing many children to glory (Heb. 2:10).

Within this pattern of contrasts, we can assimilate the poem on two levels. First, this poem shows the imprint of its origin as a poem intended for children. Every stanza contains at least one reference to infancy and children, and even the vision of heavenly glory keeps the focus on children. This is a Christmas poem for children about a child.

At a more detailed level, we can analyze how woven into the texture of the poem is a juxtaposition of the humble and the exalted, in keeping with the paradoxical nature of the incarnation. For example, the details in the opening stanza are nearly all homely, but all of this deprivation is occurring in the *city* (not the shed or even village) of royal David. Similarly, in the second stanza, everything is *poor, and meek, and lowly* except for the declaration that the person in the cradle is *God and Lord of all.* The vision of heavenly glory in the second half is mainly exalted and transcendent, but Christ is still identified as *that Child so dear and gentle,* and his throne is surrounded by children.

Poems and hymns have what is called a reception history, or the story of what happened to the text as the years have unfolded. This Christmas hymn received its highest honor in 1919, when the director of what became a worldwide Christmas service called Nine Lessons and Carols chose "Once in Royal David's City" as the processional hymn at the start of the service. It has maintained that hallowed role for over a century.[6]

The devotional takeaways from this poem are multiple. We should allow the poem to awaken the child within, as Jesus commanded (Matt. 18:3). We can contemplate anew the sacrifice represented by the humble circumstances of Christ's birth, and we can rejoice in the exaltation of Christ and of us in him.

This hymnic poem is built around the motif of divine humility that leads to ultimate exaltation. The Christ hymn in Philippians 2 follows the same pattern: "Being found in human form, [Christ] humbled himself by becoming obedient to the point of death, even death on a cross. Therefore God has highly exalted him and bestowed on him the name that is above every name" (vv. 8–9).

7

As with Gladness Men of Old

WILLIAM CHATTERTON DIX (1837–1898)

As with gladness men of old
Did the guiding star behold;
As with joy they hailed its light,
Leading onward, beaming bright;
So, most gracious God, may we
Evermore be led to thee.

As with joyful steps they sped
To that lowly cradle bed,
There to bend the knee before
Him whom heaven and earth adore;
So may we with willing feet
Ever seek thy mercy-seat.

As they offered gifts most rare
At that cradle rude and bare;
So may we with holy joy,
Pure, and free from sin's alloy,
All our costliest treasures bring,
Christ, to thee, our heavenly King.

Holy Jesus, every day
Keep us in the narrow way;
And, when earthly things are past,
Bring our ransomed souls at last
Where they need no star to guide,
Where no clouds thy glory hide.

In the heavenly country bright
Need they no created light;
Thou its Light, its Joy, its Crown,
Thou its Sun which goes not down;
There forever may we sing
Alleluias to our King.

No Christmas hymn attempts to cover the entire Christmas story. Instead, an author chooses a specific event and a cast of characters from the menu of options that the nativity story offers. Once the subject has been selected, the first order of business is to compose the scene (imagine oneself present at the place and event). Having imagined the scene, the poet moves to the meaning and application that the original event holds for us.

"As with Gladness Men of Old" is about the journey of the wise men. Instead of first reliving the journey and then extracting its significance for us, William Chatterton Dix (1837–1898) cleverly combines them in each of the first three stanzas. He does so by means of simile or analogy. Each of these stanzas begins with the conjunction *as*. Having elaborated some aspect of the wise men's journey, the analogy is then completed with a clause beginning with the conjunction *so*. The logic of the equation is "as the wise men" did, "so may we" do something comparable in our situations.

Stanza by stanza, this unfolds as follows. (1) As the wise men were led by a star to the cradle of the Christ child, we should seek to be led to God. (2) As the wise men worshiped the infant Jesus, we should worship God and seek his mercy seat. (3) As the wise men offered gifts,

23

it is only appropriate that we should bring our costliest treasures in submission to God. The three *so may we* statements are simultaneously (1) a petitionary prayer to God that he will bring it to pass, (2) a wish on our part that it will happen, and (3) self-exhortation to ourselves to make sure that it does happen.

The final two stanzas spring multiple surprises on us. The first is that the pattern of *as . . . so* statements is replaced by two stanzas of prayer addressed to Jesus. The scene likewise shifts from the nativity to the heavenly realm that awaits us in the afterlife. Interesting things happen to the light imagery as well. At the outset of the poem, the physical light of the guiding star was welcomed as the thing that led the wise men to God. In the last two stanzas, physical light is dismissed as no longer necessary because Jesus is the only light needed in heaven.

The last two stanzas are among the most beautiful in English poetry and hymnody. The first one is a prayer that Jesus will keep us on the narrow way that leads to heaven, and then, on the premise that the prayer has been granted, the last stanza is a celebration of the splendor of Jesus as we will experience it in heaven. The verbal beauty and rapturous sentiments cannot be surpassed.[7]

———

This poem invites continuous application as we progress through it, and each stanza gives us something to carry away as a devotional nugget.

———

This poem was written on a day when Dix was ill and bedridden. He read the story of the wise men in Matthew's Gospel, fell asleep, woke up, and wrote the poem before the day was over. Here is the passage that gave rise to the hymn: "Behold, wise men from the east came to Jerusalem, saying, 'Where is he who has been born king of the Jews? For we saw his star when it rose and have come to worship him'" (Matt. 2:1–2).

8

Hark! The Herald Angels Sing

CHARLES WESLEY (1707–1788)

Hark! The herald angels sing,
"Glory to the newborn King;
Peace on earth, and mercy mild,
God and sinners reconciled!"
Joyful, all ye nations, rise,
Join the triumph of the skies;
With the angelic host proclaim,
"Christ is born in Bethlehem!"

Christ, by highest heaven adored,
Christ, the everlasting Lord!
Late in time behold him come,
Offspring of the Virgin's womb.
Veiled in flesh the Godhead see;
Hail the incarnate Deity,
Pleased as man with men to dwell,
Jesus, our Emmanuel.

Hail, the heaven-born Prince of Peace!
Hail, the Sun of Righteousness!
Light and life to all he brings,
Risen with healing in his wings.
Mild he lays his glory by,

Born that man no more may die,
Born to raise the sons of earth,
Born to give them second birth.

Refrain
Hark! The herald angels sing,
"Glory to the newborn King."

———

The opening line of this hymnic poem—even the opening word—is a stroke of genius. When we read or hear the exclamation *Hark!* (meaning "Listen!"), it is as though someone next to us has grabbed our arm. Then we are told what we are hearing, and it is not something ordinary but supernatural. By means of this simple summons to listen, we are transported to the very moment when the angels began to sing. With our attention thus captivated, the rest of the opening stanza repeats the content of the angels' song and commands us to join the musical celebration.

The circumstances surrounding this poem's origin are nearly as famous as the hymn itself. Charles Wesley titled it "Hymn for Christmas-Day" because he was inspired to write it after hearing church bells while walking to a London church on Christmas morning a year after his conversion. Wesley's original opening line famously read, "Hark, how all the welkin rings." Even if we know that *welkin* is an archaic word meaning "sky" or "vault of heaven," we can be grateful to Wesley's friend George Whitefield for changing the line (and also for giving us the beautiful epithet *the newborn King* in the second line).

The opening stanza might lead us to expect that the entire poem will deal with the angels' song, but as we move beyond the first stanza, we discern that the angels' song as recreated in stanza 1 is only the launching pad for a more wide-ranging meditation on the incarnation of Christ. The middle stanza combines two elements—a rehearsal of the facts of the incarnation and an implied praise and exaltation of the incarnate Christ. The exaltation is achieved partly by the epithets (titles) for Christ—*the everlasting Lord*, for example, and *offspring of the Virgin's womb.* The concluding stanza begins with two lines that salute or *hail* the incarnate Christ, and then the rest of the stanza is a catalog of the acts of salvation that Christ's coming achieved.

Nearly every line in this poem alludes to one or more famous Bible passages. For purposes of illustration, the opening line of the concluding stanza refers to Isaiah 9:6, which calls the coming Messiah *Prince of Peace*, while the second and fourth lines quote from the prediction in Malachi 4:2 that "the sun of righteousness shall rise with healing in its wings."

The verbal beauty, well-turned phrases, and lyric exuberance of this hymnic poem should be allowed to enhance rather than obscure that it is laden with theological exposition about the incarnation. In fact, the poem is a primer (statement of first principles) on what the incarnation is and the redemption it achieved.[8]

The takeaway from this devotional text is to remind ourselves of the facts of the incarnation and to channel this knowledge into gratitude to God.

Wesley's hymn is an ever-flowing fountain of exuberance about the birth and incarnation of Jesus, and of what these mean for our salvation. Paul's declaration in Romans 5:11 expresses this "purpose statement" in kernel form: "We also rejoice in God through our Lord Jesus Christ, through whom we have now received reconciliation."

9

O Little Town of Bethlehem

PHILLIPS BROOKS (1835–1893)

O little town of Bethlehem,
How still we see thee lie;
Above thy deep and dreamless sleep
The silent stars go by;
Yet in thy dark streets shineth
The everlasting light;
The hopes and fears of all the years
Are met in thee tonight.

For Christ is born of Mary;
And gathered all above,
While mortals sleep, the angels keep
Their watch of wondering love.
O morning stars together
Proclaim the holy birth;
And praises sing to God the King,
And peace to men on earth.

How silently, how silently
The wondrous gift is given!
So God imparts to human hearts
The blessings of his heaven.
No ear may hear his coming,

But in this world of sin,
Where meek souls will receive him still,
The dear Christ enters in.

O holy Child of Bethlehem,
Descend to us, we pray;
Cast out our sin, and enter in,
Be born in us today.
We hear the Christmas angels
The great glad tidings tell;
O come to us, abide with us,
Our Lord Emmanuel.

Some Christmas hymns focus on Mary and her baby, others on the angels and their song, others on the wise men and their journey. Our repertoire of Christmas hymns would be incomplete without one that celebrates the humble town where Jesus was born. "O Little Town of Bethlehem" fills the niche with distinction.

It also falls into the category of hymns whose origin is as captivating as the hymn. Phillips Brooks, the author of this hymnic poem, was rector of a church located on a corner of Rittenhouse Square in Philadelphia. In 1865 he took a trip to the Holy Land, and during the days surrounding Christmas he found himself in Jerusalem. After dinner on Christmas Eve, he mounted a horse and made the two-hour trip to Bethlehem. On the way into town, he passed the field where the shepherds are reputed to have heard the angels. Three years later, when Brooks wanted a new song for the children in his congregation to sing, his memory went back to his Christmas Eve visit to Bethlehem, and his imagination led to one of the world's favorite Christmas songs.

Strictly speaking, only the first two stanzas are about the town of Bethlehem, but they are so beautiful and evocative that we rightly think of the poem as being about the town where Jesus was born. Brooks's first goal is to lead us to be present in our imaginations in Bethlehem on the night of Jesus's birth there. In addition to setting the scene, these stanzas remind us of the agents and events that made up the birth of Jesus. Already in these stanzas Brooks also gives us hints of the deeper spiritual meanings of what happened in Bethlehem on the night of the nativity.

The second half of the poem leaves the literal Bethlehem behind and moves to a spiritual place of coming. In stanza 3, Jesus is pictured as coming not to Bethlehem but *to human hearts* that receive him as Savior. This is a silent coming, not the coming accompanied by miraculous signs and wonders that occurred when Jesus was born in Bethlehem.

To recap, by the time we reach the final stanza we have relived the first Christmas in Bethlehem and pondered the possibility and wonder that Jesus can silently enter the souls of people who receive him. The final stanza is a prayer addressed to the *holy Child of Bethlehem*, an epithet that keeps the motif of Bethlehem alive in our awareness. With stanza 3 having asserted the possibility of Christ's coming to individual souls, the concluding stanza prays that it will be true in our own lives. Six petitions comprise this moving prayer. The last line is a perfect summation of the poem: *Our Lord Emmanuel.*[9]

There is no more moving Christmas hymn than this one, and the way to claim its affective richness is to allow the beauty of the words and sentiments to calm our spirits.

"O Little Town of Bethlehem" immortalizes the humble town of Bethlehem on the basis of the world-changing event of Jesus's birth there. The simple, understated report in Luke 2:4, 6–7 awakens the same feeling of awe: "Joseph also went up from Galilee . . . to . . . Bethlehem. . . . And while they were there, the time came for [Mary] to give birth. And she gave birth to her firstborn son and wrapped him in swaddling cloths and laid him in a manger."

10

Silent Night

JOSEF MOHR (1792–1846)

Silent night! Holy night!
All is calm, all is bright
Round yon virgin mother and child.
Holy infant, so tender and mild,
Sleep in heavenly peace.

Silent night! Holy night!
Shepherds quake at the sight!
Glories stream from heaven afar,
Heavenly hosts sing "Alleluia,
Christ the Savior is born!"

Silent night! Holy night!
Son of God, love's pure light
Radiant beams from thy holy face,
With the dawn of redeeming grace,
Jesus, Lord at thy birth.

———

Time magazine boldly declared on the basis of a survey that "Silent Night" is "the most popular Christmas song ever." Originally written in German, it has been translated into more than three hundred languages. Many a Christmas service begins with the foot-tapping exuberance of "Joy to the World," but it is even more predictable that services will end with "Silent Night." There is a reason for this phenomenon, as we will see.

One reason for the success of this poem is that it keeps its focus on just one thing. As the opening line of every stanza clearly states, this poem is about the *night* of Jesus's birth. The primary spiritual quality that Josef Mohr (1792–1846) ascribes to the night is that it is *holy*—set apart from all other nights in the history of the world. As a tribute to its holiness, the night is also declared to be *silent*. Through the centuries, poets have stressed the silence of the night of the nativity as a way of expressing reverence and awe at the birth of God in human form.

With the holiness and symbolic silence of the night as a constant background, each stanza makes its own contribution to the meditation on the night of Christ's birth. The first stanza transports us in our imagination to the manger scene. After setting a hushed atmosphere of calm and brightness, the last line of this stanza leads us to address the Christ child directly, wishing or commanding him to *sleep in heavenly peace*.

The middle stanza keeps us in our imagination at the holy night of the nativity, but the scene that we experience is a foil or contrast to the calm manger scene of the preceding stanza. Now the supernatural splendor of the angels makes the shepherds tremble in fear. The artistic category of the picturesque in stanza 1 is replaced by the sublime in stanza 2. Both were part of the holy night of Christ's birth.

After the first two stanzas have transported us to the first Christmas, the final stanza turns us in prayer to Jesus. It is a prayer of adoration as we realize that the events we have been contemplating are nothing less than *the dawn of redeeming grace*. While there have been hints of light in the first two stanzas, light explodes in this stanza with the images of *pure light, radiant beams*, and *dawn*.[10]

Why have Christians so uniformly gravitated to "Silent Night" as the right hymn with which to end a Christmas Eve service? The answer lies in its quality of calm and repose. Many Greek statues are famous for their sense of repose, with every detail adding to the effect of harmony and rest. That is what "Silent Night" conveys. It leads us to rest in the beauty and peace of the night of Jesus's birth.

———

The nativity story of Luke 2 is permeated with the same sense of calm and repose as this hymnic poem is: "And [the shepherds] went with haste and found Mary and Joseph, and the baby lying in a manger" (v. 16). All is calm in the scene.

PART 2

CLASSIC PROSE
DEVOTIONALS

The Christmas devotionals in this section come to us in the form of prose rather than poetry. But as the word *classic* hints, they are not exactly like the expository prose devotional that encompasses most published devotionals today. They possess qualities that raise them to a realm that is half prose and half poetic.

What makes these ten texts classic rather than ordinary? The authors, first of all. They are a roll call of famous Christian leaders through the centuries. They are not classic authors because they are famous but the reverse—they became famous because of their superior qualities and their elevated roles in the history of Christianity. As we look at the list of names, we just naturally want to know what they have to impart to us about Christmas and the incarnation.

Great classic prose does not use as many distinctive devices of expression as poetry does, but it uses *some* of the same resources. Poets are more imaginative than most people are—better at picturing scenes and events and rendering them in concrete rather than abstract ways. The authors represented in these selections had superior powers of imagination. The imagination is always on the lookout for original insights and fresh angles of vision, and this too characterizes the selections in Part 2. The authors whose works become classics find ways to overcome the overly familiar, the trite, the platitudinous.

Part of this knack consists of seeing what is paradoxical in a subject—something apparently contradictory that upon analysis is seen to be true. Sometimes a classic prose devotional challenges a conventional viewpoint. Or there may simply be something dissonant—something that does not quite seem to fit—something that requires analysis and an adjustment in our thinking.

On a stylistic level too classic prose rises above the utilitarian level of everyday discourse. Verbal beauty is one aspect of this stylistic flair. Classic prose possesses some of the succinctness of expression that sets poetry apart from ordinary prose. Often verbal beauty and conciseness produce an aphoristic quality—the quality of being striking and memorable the way a proverb is.

The authors included in this section wrote on many aspects of the nativity and incarnation. I selected passages with a view toward covering all of the main aspects of Christmas, parceled out among the authors.

11

Mary, Our Example

JOHN CALVIN (1509–1564)

And Elizabeth was filled with the Holy Spirit, and she exclaimed, . . . "Blessed is she who believed that there would be a fulfillment of what was spoken to her from the Lord." And Mary said, "My soul magnifies the Lord, and my spirit has rejoiced in God my Savior." (Luke 1:41–42, 45–47)

Here Elizabeth indicates the real reason why Mary is to be praised: it is because she was obedient to the word which the angel brought her. That, then, is the essential quality we ought to note about Mary. We should not judge according to our own estimate or understanding, but according to the truth which Elizabeth utters in the power of the Holy Spirit. . . .

Although this passage is about the Virgin Mary, it is relevant to each and every one of us. Here we have God declaring [through Elizabeth] that Mary is blessed because she believes. By that he means that if we trust in his promises and firmly cling to them, if we make them the ground of our salvation, our happiness is complete. . . .

How is it possible for us to rejoice in God? The Virgin Mary supplies us with the answer when she says "in God my Savior." That is where our joy begins—with the assurance that God is for us a Savior. . . . To rejoice in God is impossible until we experience the love he has for us, and until we know that he will not desert us but will lead us on to the end. . . . To sum up, from Mary we learn that, to praise God, we first need faith, and that we are moved to praise by the assurance of his good will toward us. . . .

Observe what little value Mary attaches to herself. If we would pay her appropriate honor, we must be of the same mind as she. . . . [Catholics] hail her as Queen of heaven, Star to guide the wanderer, Salvation of the world, Hope and Light of day. . . . The very opposite is true! The higher God raised Mary, the more clearly she shows how Christ is to be magnified and exalted. . . .

The greatest praise we can render Mary is to take her as our teacher; she must instruct us, and we will be her pupils. . . . We must follow her example, and remember that God looked on her with pity. She should be to us a mirror of God's mercy. For in mercy God chose us for himself, sinners though we were, rescued us from the abyss of death and had compassion on us. Mary is thus set before us as an example to imitate. With her we acknowledge that we . . . are utterly reliant on God's goodness. That is how we can be Mary's pupils, proving by our aptness that we have been attentive to her teaching.

What higher honor can we confer on her than that? From Mary's song we learn that she bore Jesus Christ, in his human nature, not only in her womb but in her heart—in all her affections and in her understanding. . . . Following her example, we should praise God and learn to rejoice in him. There is no greater blessing than the gospel's assurance that God desires to be reconciled to us, not imputing our sins to us but fully absolving us in Jesus' name. . . . We should continually rejoice in God and hope in him, since he has been so generous and merciful toward us. . . . In his mercy alone we will find blessing, happiness and salvation.

John Calvin (1509–1564) was a leading light of the Protestant Reformation and one of the most influential Christians of all time. He was both a preacher and theologian, and the excerpt presented here bears the imprint of both. Calvin's meditation on Mary the mother of Jesus has been placed first in this section because it illustrates to perfection certain principles of biblical interpretation that underlie all of the entries in this anthology.

Before we turn to these principles, we should pay attention to the meditation that Calvin has composed on the mother of Jesus. There is a corrective agenda at work in Calvin's thoughts. In the background lies the Roman Catholic elevation of Mary to a semi-divine status. As a Protestant theologian, Calvin wants to steer his readers away from such heresy. His persuasive strategy is to mention the abuse in passing so it is on our radar screen, and then to lavish his attention on a correct understanding of Mary. But there is a more subtle revisionist agenda at work as well. Even if we do not elevate Mary to a divine level, our immediate tendency is to think of Mary's uniqueness and separateness from average people. We don't intend to elevate Mary above common humanity, but how can we ignore that she is unique in human history, the one whose virgin conception brought Jesus into the world?

Calvin seeks to reverse this way of thinking. He offers us Mary as "one of us"—someone whose example of faith is completely available for us to imitate. The best way to honor Mary, says Calvin, is not to put her on a pedestal but to follow her example.

Hidden in Calvin's meditation are some epoch-making principles of biblical and literary interpretation. One is the principle of *representative action*. This means that the characters and events in a biblical text (in this case the Christmas story) represent meanings and principles beyond themselves. This overlaps with the second principle of *universality*, by which is meant that we can find our own experiences in the events and characters in the Christmas story. Thirdly, and again overlapping the other principles, is what in Calvin's era was called *example theory*. This means that the way literary and biblical texts convey their meanings is by embodying truth in *examples* of virtue, vice, and other experiences. Calvin himself states the key principle: *Although this passage is about the Virgin Mary, it is relevant to each and every one of us.*

All of the selections in this Christmas anthology are based on the premise that the details in the Bible's nativity story actually happened

39

to real-life people. But none of the authors stops there. They all find universal principles in the original facts that apply to us. In the Christmas story preeminently, the literal details carry metaphoric or symbolic overtones. That there was no room in the inn for Jesus, for example, is a picture of how fallen humanity lives without God's intervening grace.[11]

———

In applying this meditation, we should first absorb Calvin's moving thoughts on Mary and relish the beautiful language in which they are expressed. Then we can allow the principles of interpretation that Calvin states inform our understanding of all the devotionals in this anthology.

———

Calvin offers us Mary as an example of how to experience Christmas the right way. Luke 2:19, part of the Christmas story, gives us a snapshot of Mary as a model of treasuring and meditating on the truth about Jesus: "But Mary treasured up all these things, pondering them in her heart."

12

Bethlehem, the Town
God Chose

BERNARD OF CLAIRVAUX (1090–1153)

Jesus Christ, the Son of God, is born in Bethlehem of Judah.
What heart [is] so stony as not to be softened at these words?
. . . What announcement could be sweeter? What intelligence
more enrapturing? Was its like ever heard before? Or when
did the world ever receive such tidings? . . . So overpowering is
the music of this short speech that it loses melody if one iota is
changed. . . .

In all the wide world, Bethlehem, thy name is now celebrated,
and all generations call thee blessed. Everywhere glorious things
are said of thee, O little city of God. Everywhere is sung, A man
is born in her, and the Most High himself hath founded her.

Behold what condescension! It is not in the royal city of Jerusalem, but in Bethlehem, which is the least of the thousands of
Judah. O Bethlehem! O little Bethlehem, once little, now magnified by the Lord! He has magnified thee Who, though great,
became little in thee.

Rejoice, O Bethlehem, and make holiday in thy streets with
songs of Alleluia! What city on hearing of thy good fortune
will not envy thee that most precious stable and the glory of its
manger? . . . Everywhere it is proclaimed, everywhere it is made

known that Jesus Christ, the Son of God, is born in Bethlehem of Judah. . . .

And we have no need to inquire whether anything good can come from Bethlehem. It is sufficient for us to know that our Lord willed to be born there. For doubtless there were in the world noble palaces which He might have judged worthy of His choice—palaces where the King of Glory might have been received more honorably. But it was not to purchase them that He came from His royal throne. In His left hand were riches and glory; in His right hand length of days. There was an endless supply of these treasures in heaven, but poverty could not be found there. Earth abounded and superabounded in this kind of merchandise [i.e., poverty], and men knew not its value.

The Son of God was desirous of it. He came down from heaven to make it His own, and so render it precious to us by His choice. Adorn thy bridal-chamber, O Zion, devout soul, but with humility, but with poverty. These are the swathing-bands that please our Infant Jesus; these are the rich robes in which Mary tells us He loves to be clothed. . . .

Remember, too, that it is in Bethlehem of Judah that Jesus is born, and be very careful lest you fail to be found there, lest He fail to be received by you. Bethlehem is the house of bread; Judah signifies confession or praise. If, then, you replenish your soul with the food of the Divine Word, . . . and devoutly receive the Bread which came down from heaven, and which giveth life to the world; . . . if, moreover, you live by faith, . . . then, indeed, you are become a Bethlehem fitted to receive our Lord.

Bernard of Clairvaux (1090–1153) was a Catholic monk affiliated with Clairvaux Abbey in France. He was a poet as well as a theologian, and in that role he authored such famous hymns as "Jesus, Thou Joy of Loving Hearts" and "Jesus, the Very Thought of Thee." The poet is fully evident in the passage printed here, which fits the standard literary category known as *poetic prose* (also called prose poetry).

The places of the nativity are an essential part of the story, and none is more famous than Bethlehem. Of course there are contrary aspects and interpretations of Bethlehem. Martin Luther famously scolded Bethlehem for not finding room for Mary and her baby, saying at one point, "Shame on you, wretched Bethlehem!"

Bernard of Clairvaux with equal rhetorical flourish paints a picture of Bethlehem as the village on which God's benediction fell on the night of the nativity. There can be no doubt that Bethlehem has held a hallowed place in the history of Christianity because of Christ's birth there. We should note two aspects of Bernard's thoughts on Bethlehem. One is the reason he finds Bethlehem such a blessed town. The other is the rhetorical and poetic means by which Bernard expresses his rapturous praise of Bethlehem.

Regarding the town of Bethlehem, it is not the physical place that elicits Bernard's enthusiasm and inspires our devotion. Bernard stresses its insignificance in itself, being a place of poverty. Bernard manages his encomium or praise in such a way that we are left in no doubt that Bethlehem's claim to fame is that God chose it, not in spite of its poverty but because of that poverty. In a challenge to conventional thinking, Bernard claims that God desires and values poverty, not wealth and privilege. The praise that Bernard heaps on the town is really a way of praising Jesus and the redemption that he brought by his incarnation.

How does the author manage his feat of rhapsody? We note first the all-out quality of Bernard's praise. This quality, in turn, is based on what rhetoricians or experts of style call *superlatives*. In virtually every sentence, Bethlehem is declared to be the absolute best. Additionally, Bernard uses the rhetoric of reversal in which the qualities that the world thinks unworthy, such as poverty and the socially low, are said to be what God desires and values. Bernard manages his meditation in such a way that Bethlehem is seen to embody a grand reversal of values. Finally, in the last paragraph, Bethlehem assumes a symbolic or metaphoric quality. On the strength of its being the place to which Jesus came to earth, our own hearts are a metaphoric Bethlehem in which, if we meet the requirement of faith, Christ will be born.[12]

As we leave Bernard's rhapsody on Bethlehem, we can resolve to make Bethlehem sacred in our thinking and in our Christmas celebration, and to rectify our scale of values. Additionally, we can heed Bernard's exhortation to make our heart a Bethlehem where Jesus is born.

———

Bernard's exaltation of Bethlehem has a biblical precedent in the messianic prophecy found in Micah 5:2:

> But you, O Bethlehem Ephrathah,
>   who are too little to be among the clans of Judah,
> from you shall come forth for me
>   one who is to be ruler in Israel,
> whose coming forth is from of old,
>   from ancient days.

13

Journeying with the Wise Men

LANCELOT ANDREWES (1555–1626)

Behold, there came wise men from the East to Jerusalem, Saying, Where is He that is born King of the Jews? For we have seen His star in the East, and are come to worship Him. (Matthew 2:1–2)

The wise men sat not still gazing on the star. . . . Their seeing made them come, come a great journey. . . . The distance of the place they came from . . . was not hard [i.e., close] by as the shepherds—but [i.e., only] a step to Bethlehem over the fields; this was riding many a hundred miles . . . , through deserts, all the way waste and desolate. . . . [Finally] we consider the time of their coming, the season of the year. It was no summer progress. A cold coming they had of it at this time of the year, just the worst time of the year to take a journey, and specially a long journey. The ways deep, the weather sharp, the days short, the sun farthest off, in . . . the very dead of winter. . . .

And these difficulties they overcame, of a wearisome, irksome, troublesome, dangerous, unseasonable journey; and [i.e., despite] all this, they came. And came cheerfully and quickly as appeareth by the speed they made. . . .

And we, what should we have done? Sure these men of the East will rise in judgment against the men of the West, that is with us, and their faith against ours in this point. . . . Our fashion is to see and see again before we stir a foot, especially if it be to the worship of Christ. . . . And when we do it, we must be allowed leisure. . . . We love to make no great haste. . . .

Second, set down this: that to find where He is, we must learn to ask where He is, which we full little set ourselves to do. If we stumble on Him, so it is; but for any asking we trouble not ourselves. . . .

And now we have found where [the infant is], what then? It is neither in seeking nor finding; the end of all, the cause of all is . . . to worship Him. That is all in all, and without it all our seeing, coming, seeking, and finding is to no purpose. . . .

There now remains nothing but to include ourselves, and bear our part with [the wise men], and with the angels, and all who this day adored him. What was the loadstar of the Magi, and what were they? Gentiles. So are we. But if it must be ours, then we are to go with them. . . .

Then we have our part in it no less, nay full out as much as they. It will bring us whither it brought them, to Christ, who at His second appearing in glory will call forth these wise men, and all who have ensued the steps of their faith . . . ; for I have seen their star shining and showing forth itself by the like beams; and as they came to worship Me, so am I come to do them worship. . . . And as they offered to Me, so I am come to bestow on them, and to reward them with endless joy and bliss in My heavenly Kingdom.

Lancelot Andrewes (1555–1626) was a famous Anglican preacher of the Renaissance era. He was a court preacher, and served as head of the translation committee of the King James Version that met at Westminster Abbey in London (with the other two committees meeting at Oxford and Cambridge Universities). Andrewes is famous for his Christmas sermons, and part of that fame stems from the fact that poet T. S. Eliot quoted verbatim from this sermon in the opening lines of his poem "Journey of the Magi."

Andrewes's meditation on the journey of the wise men is based on a threefold paradigm that is nearly inevitable in Christmas meditations on the nativity story of the Bible. The first phase is to imagine oneself present at an event that happened at the nativity, picturing it as concretely as possible. Then we are led to subject the characters and event to analysis, extracting its spiritual significance. At the end we reach a moment of application and resolution as we are prompted to a specific spiritual action. This is the pattern that Andrewes follows.

His first task is to situate us in the literal, physical circumstances of the wise men's journey. We are led to see that the wise men undertook their journey immediately after they saw the star. It was a long journey, undertaken in the cold of winter. Andrewes wants us to relive the event as fully as possible by means of our imaginations.

But reliving an event is only the starting point of a Christmas meditation. So Andrewes next analyzes what spiritual principles are embodied in the journey of the wise men. He first makes something of their promptness, and that, in turn, prompts him to a satiric putdown of our own tendency toward comfort and lethargy in pursuing spiritual matters. If the journey of the wise men is thus metaphoric of how to be intentional about seeking Christ, so is their worship of Jesus when they find him.

Having journeyed with the wise men and pondered the religious meaning of their journey, in the concluding two paragraphs Andrewes offers an action plan and gives an incentive for doing it. First he commands us to do what the wise men did in seeking and worshiping Jesus. Then he springs a surprise ending on us. If we seek and find Jesus, Christ will seek and find us at his second coming. If we offer him our best, he will bestow an eternal kingdom on us.[13]

The whole meditation, and the moving conclusion especially, makes it easy for us to leave the devotional with a resolve to give our all to Jesus, knowing that our reward will be very great.

The text on which Andrewes builds his highly imaginative meditation is the following simple narrative:

> When they saw the star, they rejoiced exceedingly with great joy. And going into the house, they saw the child with Mary his mother, and they fell down and worshiped him. (Matt. 2:10–11)

14

The Paradoxes of
the Incarnation

AUGUSTINE (354–430)

He who had brought all things into existence, was brought into existence in the midst of all things. He made the day—He came into the light of day. He who was before time, set His seal upon time. Christ the Lord was forever without beginning with the Father; but look what He is today! It is His birthday. Whose birthday? The Lord's. He has a birthday? Yes, He has. . . . If He had not been begotten as a human being, we would not attain our divine rebirth; for He was born that we might be reborn. . . .

His mother carried Him in her womb; let us carry Him in our hearts. By the Incarnation of Christ was a virgin made fruitful; let our breasts be made fruitful by the faith of Christ. She gave birth to the Savior; let us give birth to good deeds. . . .

When we say, "He was born of a virgin," this is something extraordinary, you marvel. He is God! You must not marvel. Let our surprise yield to thanksgiving. Have faith; believe, for this really so happened. . . . He deigned to become man; what more do you ask? Is it not enough that God has been humbled for you? He who was God was made man. . . .

In His birth of a mother, Christ became manifest in weakness; but, born of His Father, He shows His great majesty. Among time-bound days He has His day in time; but He Himself is the Eternal Day. . . .

He lies in a manger, but He holds the world. He nurses at His mother's breasts, but He feeds the angels. He is wrapped in swaddling clothes, but He gives us the garment of immortality. He is given milk, but at the same time is adored. He finds no room at the inn, but He builds a temple for Himself in the hearts of those who believe.

That infirmity might be made strong, strength has been made weak. Let us, therefore, admire the more His human birth instead of looking down upon it; and let us in His presence try to realize the abasement that He in all His majesty accepted for our sakes. And then let us be kindled with love, that we may come to His eternity. . . .

In that bridal chamber, that is, in the Virgin's womb, His divine nature united itself to the human; and thus *the Word was made flesh* for us, that, proceeding from a mother, it might *dwell among us*; that, going before to the Father, it might prepare a place for us in which to dwell. Let us, therefore, joyfully and solemnly celebrate this day; and through the Eternal One who was born for us in time, let us faithfully long for the day eternal. . . . Let us, all of us, one heart and soul, with chaste hearts and holy desires, celebrate the birthday of the Lord.

Most of the prose authors represented in this section wrote so much about the nativity and incarnation that individual books have been published containing their most famous Christmas writings. One such book is Augustine's *Sermons for Christmas and Epiphany*. Obviously Augustine's (354–430) thoughts on the paradoxes of the incarnation are only one aspect of his Christmas writings.

Before we look at Augustine's paradoxes of Christmas, we should note his importance as someone who lived through the great change in religious thinking that occurred in the Western world when Christianity replaced ancient paganism as the ruling thought system. Augustine himself has recorded his breakthrough encounter with the idea of the incarnation. He had been raised on classical philosophy and mythology. When he read the prologue to John's Gospel, everything initially seemed familiar because John had imitated the language of familiar pagan writing, including a hymn to Zeus that Greeks had been reciting for centuries. To speak of God as a divine word (*logos*) was familiar to the classical mindset. But as Augustine kept reading, he was shocked by the sudden infusion of something new: "The Word became flesh and dwelt among us" (John 1:14). This, writes Augustine, is something that the philosophers had not taught him. The Christmas season is an excellent time for us to allow the shock of the incarnation to seize our imagination as we seek to realize the fact of deity becoming human.

Turning to the meditation printed here, it is in the very nature of the incarnation to be paradoxical. There is no other way to express the phenomenon of Christ being both divine and human. A paradox is an apparent contradiction that, upon analysis, can be seen to be true. In other words, a paradox needs to be resolved. It is akin to the genre of the riddle in needing to be "figured out."

Three motifs converge in Augustine's meditation on the incarnation. One is that Augustine has collected some striking paradoxes of the incarnation. It is our task to ponder these seeming contradictions and determine how both halves of the equation are true. Secondly, Augustine the preacher is fully evident in the passage, as he intermittently exhorts us toward religious actions, such as fruitfulness in good works and being kindled in love for Christ. Thirdly, we should relish Augustine's gift for metaphor, as when he sees an analogy between Mary's carrying Jesus in her womb and our carrying him in our hearts.[14]

As we cast a retrospective look at Augustine's meditation on the incarnation, we can resolve to allow the paradoxes of the incarnation to be a permanent part of how we understand the incarnation and to heed Augustine's prompts toward a proper devotional attitude toward Christmas.

In the spirit of Augustine's emphasis on the paradoxes of the incarnation, 2 Corinthians 8:9 gives us the paradoxes of the rich one who is poor and the poor one who is rich:

> For you know the grace of our Lord Jesus Christ, that though he was rich, yet for your sake he became poor, so that you by his poverty might become rich.

15

A Christmas Prayer

FROM LESSONS AND CAROLS

Beloved in Christ,
this Christmas Eve it is our duty and delight
to prepare ourselves to hear again the message of the angels,
and to go in heart and mind to Bethlehem,
and see this thing which is come to pass,
and the Babe lying in a manger.

Therefore let us hear again from Holy Scripture
the tale of the loving purposes of God from the first days of
our sin
until the glorious redemption brought us by this holy Child;
and let us make this house of prayer glad with our carols of
praise.

But first, because this of all things would rejoice Jesus' heart,
let us pray to him for the needs of the whole world, and all his
people;
for peace upon the earth he came to save;
for love and unity within the one Church he did build;
for goodwill among all peoples.

And particularly at this time let us remember
the poor, the cold, the hungry, the oppressed;
the sick and them that mourn; the lonely and the unloved;

the aged and the little children;
and all who know not the Lord Jesus, or who love him not,
or who by sin have grieved his heart of love.

Lastly let us remember all those who rejoice with us,
but upon another shore and in a greater light,
that multitude which no one can number,
whose hope was in the Word made flesh,
and with whom, in this Lord Jesus, we for evermore are one.

These prayers and praises let us humbly offer up to the throne
of heaven,
in the words that Christ himself has taught us.

> Our Father, which art in heaven,
>   hallowed be thy name,
>   thy kingdom come, thy will be done,
>   in earth as it is in heaven.
> Give us this day our daily bread.
> And forgive us our trespasses,
>   as we forgive them that trespass against us.
> And lead us not into temptation,
>   but deliver us from evil,
> for thine is the kingdom, the power, and the glory,
>   for ever and ever.
>   Amen.

The Almighty God bless us with his grace;
Christ give us the joys of everlasting life;
and unto the fellowship of the citizens above
may the King of Angels bring us all.

Surely it is unexpected that the Anglican Prayer Book does not contain a liturgy specifically designed for a Christmas service (separate from Bible readings related to Christmas, which the Prayer Book does contain). For over a century, the prayer printed here has served as an admirable "stand-in" for a formal-sounding Christmas liturgy for Christmas Eve services in the English-speaking world. It has become a hallowed Christmas text through usage and association.

A Christmas Eve service known as Lessons and Carols had its origin in 1918 at King's College Chapel, part of Cambridge University in England. Since then, the festival has been held annually around the world right to the present day, with the same basic content and format. The customary processional hymn is "Once in Royal David's City." After the procession is finished, with everyone standing, the presiding minister leads the congregation in this "bidding prayer." The whole occasion makes the prayer an electrifying experience, but even without that celebrative atmosphere, the prayer makes a moving private devotional.

The quaint term *bidding prayer* refers to a specific format for prayer in a public setting. A minister "bids" or instructs a congregation to pray for the items that he lists individually. Either the assembled people pray silently after each item is named, or the leader expresses the petitions on behalf of the congregation. In both cases, a bidding prayer uses the rhetorical formula of the command *let us. . . .*

A prayer can become a devotional reading in all the ordinary ways. It fixes our attention on spiritual reality. It directs our souls and beings directly to God as we address him. It awakens our emotions (or what past ages called "our affections"). It prompts a spirit of gratitude and devotion to God. It channels beauty of expression in a religious direction, along the lines of the King James Bible's phrase "the beauty of holiness" (1 Chron. 16:29; 2 Chron. 20:21; Pss. 29:2; 96:9). Finally, a prayer can become a devotional exercise as we ponder each petition for the uplift and edification that it yields.

To worshipers who are familiar with this bidding prayer, hearing it every year at a Christmas service is like renewing acquaintance with an esteemed friend. If we look carefully at how the prayer unfolds, we can see that it is a carefully contrived structure of surprises and retarding devices. The whole purpose of the Lessons and Carols service is to get to the lessons and carols, but this prayer holds us back, creating a sense of suspense. Paradoxically, because these units are detours from our eventual destination of lessons and carols, our attention is riveted on each holding pattern.

The style of this devotional prayer is part of its greatness. We immediately note the stately beauty of the words and lines. Like the language of the King James Bible (which doubtless influenced the composer of the prayer), the language of the bidding prayer is elegant without being stilted. We can say further that it combines simplicity with majesty.[15]

———

As we look closely at the prayer, we discern that only a relatively small part of it deals directly with Christmas. The takeaway from the prayer might therefore be to see how the proper use of Christmas is to see Christmas in all of life.

———

The spirit of expansiveness and exuberance that breathes through the prayer is infectious, as we traverse the whole world, with all its groupings, and the heavenly realm as well as the earthly. Paul's prayer in Ephesians 3:14–16 similarly sweeps us up into its orb:

> For this reason I bow my knees before the Father, from whom every family in heaven and on earth is named, that according to the riches of his glory he may grant you to be strengthened with power through his Spirit in your inner being.

16

The Greatest Birthday

CHARLES SPURGEON (1834–1892)

The angel said unto them, Fear not: for, behold, I bring
you good tidings of great joy, which shall be to all people.
(Luke 2:10)

The birth of Christ should be the subject of supreme joy. We have
the angelic warrant for rejoicing because Christ is born. It is a truth
so full of joy that it caused the angel who came to announce it to
be filled with gladness. . . . Yea, so glad were angels at this gospel
that, when the discourse was over, one angel having evangelized
and given out the gospel for the day, suddenly a band of choristers
appeared and sang an anthem loud and sweet. . . . A multitude of
the heavenly host had heard that a chosen messenger had been sent
to proclaim the new-born King, and, filled with joy and adoration,
they gathered up their strength to pursue him, for they could not let
him go to earth alone on such an errand. They overtook him just
as he had reached the last word of his discourse. . . .

The word made flesh means hope for the human race, not-
withstanding its fall. The race is not to be outlawed . . . , for,
lo, the Lord hath married into the race, and the Son of God has
become the Son of man. This is enough to make all that is within
us sing for joy. . . . Further, it is clear that if God condescends
to be so intimately allied with humankind, he intends to deliver
man, and to bless him. Incarnation prophesies salvation. . . .

When God stoops down to man, it must mean that man is to be lifted up to God. What joy there is in this! . . .

The angel further went on to give these shepherds cause for joy by telling them that while their Savior was born to be the Lord, yet he was so born in lowliness that they would find him a babe wrapped in swaddling clothes, lying in a manger. Is there cause of joy there? I say indeed there is, for it is the terror of the Godhead which keeps the sinner oftentimes away from reconciliation; but see how the Godhead hath graciously concealed itself in a babe. . . . Who ever heard of trembling in the presence of a babe? Yet is the Godhead there. . . .

Nor is this all. The angel called for joy, and I ask for it too, on this ground, that the birth of this child was to bring glory to God in the highest, on earth peace, good will toward men. The birth of Christ has given such glory to God as I know not that he could ever have had by any other means. . . .

I have shown you that there was room enough for joy to the shepherds, but you and I, who live in later days, when we understand the whole business of salvation, ought to be even more glad than they were, though they glorified and praised God for all the things that they had heard and seen. Come, my brethren, let us at least do as much as these simple shepherds, and exult with our whole souls.

Charles Haddon Spurgeon (1834–1892) of the British Victorian era is one of the most famous preachers of all time. The excerpted passage gives a glimpse of the brilliance of his thinking and mastery of words, but in addition Spurgeon was a master orator whose pulpit presence held his congregation at Metropolitan Tabernacle in London spellbound. As we assimilate the passage printed here, we should imagine ourselves present in London in a congregation of five thousand on December 24, 1876.

Spurgeon's meditation keeps the focus on the announced subject, which is why we should be supremely happy about the birth of Christ. It is a simple idea, but Spurgeon keeps unfolding more and more nuances, until we begin to think that the subject is inexhaustible. The starting point is the message of the angels to the shepherds. After telling the shepherds not to fear, the angel states reasons why the shepherds should not fear. The first reason is that the angel is bringing *tidings of great joy.* Spurgeon then follows the path of the angel's further statements, evolving a whole string of reasons why the coming of Jesus is the supreme joy. A sense of suspense builds up, as we hang on the author's words to find out what the next reason for joy is.

In addition to this genius for organization and construction, the imaginative flair of the performance makes this more than a conventional devotional. In the opening paragraph, for example, Spurgeon makes the joining of the first angel with a host of angels come alive with a fictional story. This, in turn, is enlivened by bridge-building between the original Christmas and our own day. Thus the first angel is said to have *given out the gospel for the day*, as though he were a preacher on Sunday morning. The late-arriving angels, called *a band of choristers*, are imagined as not wanting to miss out on the excitement of a trip to earth, and therefore hurrying to make it in time for the last sentence of the first angel's message.

Such imaginative touches enliven the whole passage. For example, Jesus *married into the* [human] *race.* Often these touches become aphoristic (expressed as concise and memorable statements that are impossible to forget): *incarnation prophesies salvation*; or *when God stoops down to man, it must mean that man is to be lifted up to God.* And at the end we are left with a challenge to do at least as much as the shepherds did when they exulted with their whole souls.[16]

As we leave Spurgeon's meditation, we can continue to think about how the birth of Jesus is a cause for supreme joy in our own lives and at this season of the year.

Spurgeon's goal is to lead us to tally up our reasons for being joyful at Christmastime. Paul's prayer in Romans 15:13 encapsulates that same wish:

> May the God of hope fill you with all joy and peace in believing, so that by the power of the Holy Spirit you may abound in hope.

17

Nicene Creed

(325)

I believe in one God,
    the Father Almighty,
    maker of heaven and earth,
    and of all things visible and invisible;

And in one Lord Jesus Christ,
    the only begotten Son of God,
    begotten of his Father before all worlds,
    God of God, Light of Light,
    very God of very God,
    begotten not made,
    being of one substance with the Father,
    by whom all things were made;
Who for us and for our salvation
    came down from heaven,
    and was incarnate by the Holy Spirit of the Virgin Mary,
    and was made man.
    He was crucified also for us under Pontius Pilate.
    He suffered and was buried,
    and the third day he rose again according to the Scriptures,
    and ascended into heaven,

and sits on the right hand of the Father;
he shall come again with glory
to judge both the living and the dead,
whose kingdom shall have no end.

And I believe in the Holy Spirit,
the Lord and giver of life,
who proceeds from the Father and the Son,
who with the Father and the Son together is worshiped and glorified,
who spoke by the prophets.

I believe one catholic and apostolic church.
I acknowledge one baptism for the remission of sins,
and I look for the resurrection of the dead
and the life of the world to come.

Amen.

Two avenues enable us to experience the Nicene Creed as a Christmas devotional. The first is expressed by the two formulas "Christmas in the Nicene Creed" and "the Nicene Creed in Christmas." In regard to the latter, the Nicene Creed is an unofficial Christmas creed. In some churches where the Apostles' Creed is the normal creed recited on Sunday, the Nicene Creed makes a guest appearance during the Christmas season. The explanation is that the Nicene Creed gives more extended treatment to the nature of the incarnation of Jesus.

This, in turn, relates to the origin of the Nicene Creed. It grew out of the Council of Nicaea (325), which refuted the position of Arius that Jesus was not truly divine. The result for us is that we have a creed that fully defines the incarnation and enables us to celebrate it in a special way during the Christmas season. This means, in turn, that we can find Christmas in the Nicene Creed. Our thoughts are fixed on the nature of the incarnation and the redemptive work that it made possible.

A second avenue that enables us to experience the Nicene Creed as a Christmas devotional is the principle "no cross, no cradle." The section of the creed that defines Christ's incarnate nature is followed by an extended list of his acts of redemption, beginning with the hallowed transition *who for us and for our salvation.* The incarnation and coming of Jesus to earth cannot be properly understood apart from the atonement achieved on the cross. The list of redemptive acts listed in the creed outlines the reason and purpose of the incarnation. It gives us "the rest of the story," which can easily drop out of sight with our Christmastime excitement over the thought that deity became human. The Nicene Creed tells us why Jesus became incarnate.

The content of the Nicene Creed thus adds an important theological element to our Christmas understanding, but we should also be receptive to the beauty and artistry that make this content riveting and impossible to forget. Although the Nicene Creed is a prose composition, that prose is so highly organized that it fits a literary category known as poetic prose. The most obvious poetic technique is composition by parallel lines that march in stately manner one after another. The rhythm of rising and falling language is masterful and lends itself to oral performance (though smooth rhythm is something we notice even in silent reading). And the words that make up this flow of phrases and clauses represent verbal beauty of the highest order. The Nicene Creed is simple and elegant at the same time.[17]

As we make the Nicene Creed a permanent part of our thinking, we can allow it to define the relationship of the Son to the Father and Holy Spirit, and to be a summary of essential teaching about the incarnation and atonement to which we can always return as a statement of "first things."

A brief creed embedded in 1 Timothy 3:16 is a fitting parallel to the Nicene Creed:

> He was manifested in the flesh,
> vindicated by the Spirit,
> seen by angels,
> proclaimed among the nations,
> believed on in the world,
> taken up in glory.

18

On the Incarnation

ATHANASIUS (296–373)

Being in His own nature without a body and existing as the Word, Christ has yet been manifested to us in a human body for our salvation, out of the lovingkindness and goodness of His Own Father. . . . We must speak first of the creation of the universe, and of God its Maker, in order that we may duly perceive that its re-creation has been accomplished by the same Word who originally made it. For it will not appear at all inconsistent for the Father to have accomplished its salvation in Him through whom He made it in the beginning. . . .

In speaking of the manifestation of the Savior to us, we must speak also of the origin of humankind, that you may know that our hopeless case was the reason of His coming down. . . . We were the occasion of His becoming flesh, and for our salvation He showed such lovingkindness as to be born and to appear in a human body. . . .

As, then, the human race, whom God had created rational, was wasting away, and God's noble works perishing, what was God who is good to do? Permit corruption to prevail against them, and death to hold the mastery over them? In that case, what was the use of their being made in the beginning? . . . It was impossible to leave man to be carried off by corruption, because that would be unfitting and unworthy of God's goodness. . . .

For this purpose, then, the incorporeal and incorruptible and immaterial Word of God came into our region. . . . He pitied our race and had compassion on our weakness and condescended to our corruption and took to Himself a body, one like our own. . . . Being Himself mighty, and Artificer of the universe, He prepared in the Virgin the body as a temple for Himself, and personally appropriated this as an instrument, being made known in it and dwelling in it. . . .

It was impossible for the Word to die, being immortal and the Son of the Father, so for this reason He took to Himself a body capable of death, in order that the Word who is above all might be a sufficient representative of all in the discharge of the penalty of death. . . . Thus the immortal Son of God, . . . the Word, took to Himself a body capable of death, that He might offer it as His own in place of all. . . . This indeed is the first cause of the Savior's becoming man. . . .

[The second cause is that] when people see the incarnate Image, the Word of the Father, they may be able to receive through Him a conception of the Father, and thus, coming to know their Maker, live the happy and truly blessed life. . . . When a portrait painted on a panel has disappeared as a result of staining, the person whose portrait it is needs to come and sit for it again, that the likeness may be renewed on the same material; for the sake of his picture the material itself on which it has been painted is not thrown away, but the likeness is retraced upon it. Similarly, the All-holy Son of the Father, being the Image of the Father, came into our sphere to renew man made after Himself.

Wherefore as man He comes to dwell, taking to Himself a body like the other, . . . so that they who were not willing to know Him from His providence over the universe, and from His guidance of it, may, through the works done through His body, know the Word of God in the body and through Him the Father.

In the annals of Christian theology, the name of Athanasius (296–373) is automatically linked with the incarnation. Certainly Athanasius was important for more than this. For half a century he was an important churchman and controversialist (especially in combating the heresy of Arianism). He is the first person known to have identified the twenty-seven books of the New Testament as we know it. But his greatest claim to fame is his relatively short book of 125 pages on the incarnation. No anthology of Christmas meditations is complete without its inclusion.

Athanasius has his own "take" on the incarnation, and it is doubtless his original angle that has made his treatise stand out from the conventional treatments of the subject. The first thing we need to know is that Athanasius is interested in the *logic* of the incarnation. His focus is *why* Jesus came to earth in human form. What is the logic behind it? Athanasius asks. Surely this is a welcome approach when we are looking for a meditation on the incarnation.

The excerpt here is such a compact version of Athanasius's intricate argument that it almost requires a roadmap. Several entries in this anthology marvel at the paradox of God being made in the image of man in the incarnation, and Athanasius is also interested in that. But his starting point takes a step back to the creation, with its premise of people being made in the image of God. God intended people to retain this imprint of the divine on their very nature, but the fall of the human race thwarted God's intention.

As Athanasius thinks this through, he imagines a divine dilemma, as hinted by the question in the passage here, *What was God . . . to do?* God did not wish to lose his investment. In fact, Athanasius thinks that it would be incommensurate with God's goodness to allow the human race to perish in a pit of corruption. The only way to salvage humanity was for the immortal deity to take on the human image as God had created it. This taking on of mortality enabled Jesus to die as an atoning representative of the race. The first reason for the incarnation was thus redemptive, and this is where most writing on the subject ends.

But Athanasius keeps going and adds a second reason for the incarnation. The first reason was salvific, and the second one is revelatory. The human race showed itself incapable of adequately *seeing* God through his creation and providence, so God repainted his portrait of perfect humanity by sending his Son in human form. This reveals God and perfection in a form that we can understand.[18]

Athanasius's argument on the incarnation is easily remembered, like an answer to a catechism question. Why did Jesus come in human form? To redeem us and to reveal God to us. The second of these is not as prominent in our thinking as it should be; by linking it with the first, Athanasius helps us correct our understanding.

Athanasius's twofold argument is that Jesus came in the flesh for the purposes of saving us and giving us a model to follow. Hebrews 2:17–18 follows a similar contour:

> Therefore [Jesus] had to be made like his brothers in every respect, . . . to make propitiation for the sins of the people. For because he himself has suffered when tempted, he is able to help those who are being tempted.

19

The Excellency of Christ Seen in Christmas

Jonathan Edwards (1703–1758)

In this act of taking on human nature, Christ's infinite condescension ["descending to be with"] wonderfully appeared, that he who was God should become man, that the word should be made flesh, and should take on him a nature infinitely below his original nature. And it appears yet more remarkably in the low circumstances of his incarnation: he was conceived in the womb of a poor young woman, whose poverty appeared in this, when she came to offer sacrifices of her purification, she brought what was allowed of in the law only in case of a person . . . [who] was so poor that she was not able to offer a lamb.

And though his infinite condescension thus appeared in the manner of his incarnation, yet his divine dignity also appeared in it; for though he was conceived in the womb of a poor virgin, yet he was conceived there by the power of the Holy Ghost. And his divine dignity also appeared in the holiness of his conception and birth. Though he was conceived in the womb of one of the corrupt race of mankind, yet he was conceived and born without sin. . . .

His infinite condescension marvelously appeared in the manner of his birth. He was brought forth in a stable because there was no room for them in the inn. The inn was taken up

by others who were looked upon as persons of greater account.
The Blessed Virgin, being poor and despised, was turned or
shut out. Though she was in such extreme circumstances, yet
those that counted themselves her betters would not give place
to her; and therefore, in the time of her travail, she was forced
to betake herself to a stable; and when the child was born, it
was wrapped in swaddling clothes, and laid in a manger. There
Christ lay a little infant, and there he eminently appeared as
a lamb.

But yet this feeble infant, born thus in a stable, and laid in
a manger, was born to conquer and triumph over Satan, that
roaring lion. He came to subdue the mighty powers of darkness, and make a show of them openly, and so to restore peace
on earth, and to manifest God's good-will towards men, and
to bring glory to God in the highest, according as the end of
his birth was declared by the joyful songs of the glorious hosts
of angels appearing to the shepherds at the same time that
the infant lay in the manger; whereby his divine dignity was
manifested. . . .

Though Christ dwelt in poor outward circumstances,
whereby his condescension and humility especially appeared,
and his majesty was veiled, yet his divine divinity and glory
did in many of his acts shine through the veil, and it illustri-
ously appeared, that he was not only the Son of man, but the
great God.

Thus, in the circumstances of his infancy, his outward social lowness appeared; yet there was something then to show
forth his divine dignity, in the wise men's being stirred up to
come from the east to give honor to him their being led by a
miraculous star, and coming and falling down and worship-
ping him, and presenting him with gold, frankincense, and
myrrh. . . .

Christ's incarnation was a greater and more wonderful thing
than ever had yet come to pass. The creation of the world
was a very great thing, but not so great as the incarnation of
Christ. It was a great thing for God to make the creature, but
not so great as for the Creator himself to become a creature.
. . . God becoming man was greater than all [previous events

in history]. Then the greatest person was born that ever was or ever will be.

Jonathan Edwards was one of the most important religious figures in the history of American Christianity. He was a theologian, preacher, and prolific writer. The particular contribution of the passage printed here is its balance between contrasting aspects of Christ's incarnation.

The context that best enables us to see this balance is the way in which most of the selections in this anthology emphasize either the humility seen in Christ's birth and life, or the exaltation of it, as seen in such miracles as a virgin birth and the appearance of an angelic host and the supernatural guidance of the wise men. Edwards brings both of these together, and seeing how he works this out is the key to our assimilation of the passage. As the template for this balanced picture of the incarnation, Edwards has in mind two biblical metaphors for Jesus—the lamb and the lion.

The way in which Edwards gets us to see the complementary sides of the incarnation is subtle and masterful. The main principle is that of a back-and-forth movement like a pendulum. First Edwards places data before us that demonstrates the humility of Jesus seen in his nativity and incarnation. Then the words *but* and *yet* set up a countermovement that rehearses the signs of Christ's majesty and exalted status. A few of the paragraphs are devoted exclusively to one or the other of these themes, but mainly we need to keep alert within paragraphs to see the swing of the pendulum. This is entirely appropriate, because the humility and exaltation were intertwined on the night of Jesus's birth and afterward.

Edwards repeatedly uses the word *condescension*, and we need to understand that this is a theological word and concept, with no hint of the negative connotations that the word holds in common usage today. Christ's condescension was his descent from a higher divine state to a lower human one, accompanied by his relinquishing of divine privilege in order to accomplish an action (the salvation of people) that strict justice does not require.

The final paragraph steps back from the analysis that has preceded and makes sure that we comprehend the greatness of what has been presented. Having been led to see the complementary facts of Christ's humility and greatness as seen in Christmas, at the end we are prompted to celebrate those facts.[19]

The takeaway from this meditation is that we need to see that the nativity and incarnation combine opposites (humility and exaltation), and that we need to keep an eye on both as we celebrate the season.

Jonathan Edwards based his sermon "The Excellency of Christ" on Revelation 5:5–6:

> And one of the elders said to me, "Weep no more; behold, the Lion of the tribe of Judah, the Root of David, has conquered, so that he can open the scroll and its seven seals." And between the throne and the four living creatures and among the elders I saw a Lamb standing, as though it had been slain. . . .

20

The Birth of Jesus

MARTIN LUTHER (1483–1546)

Bad enough that a young bride married only a year could not have had her baby at Nazareth in her own house instead of making all that journey of three days when heavy with child. How much worse that when she arrived there was no room for her. The inn was full. No one would release a room to this pregnant woman. She had to go to a cow stall and there bring forth the Maker of all creatures because nobody would give way. . . .

When now they were come to Bethlehem, the Evangelist says that they were, of all, the lowest and the most despised, and must make way for everyone until they were shoved into a stable to make a common lodging and table with the cattle. . . .

The birth was still more pitiable. No one regarded this young wife bringing forth her first-born. No one took her condition to heart. No one noticed that in a strange place she had not the very least thing needful in childbirth. There she was without preparation: no light, no fire, in the dead of night, in thick darkness. No one came to give the customary assistance. The guests swarming in the inn were carousing, and no one attended to this woman. . . . And now think what she could use for swaddling clothes—some garment, she could spare, perhaps her veil. . . .

She "wrapped him in swaddling clothes, and laid him in a manger." Why not in a cradle, on a bench, or on the ground?

Because they had no cradle, bench, table, board, nor anything whatever except the manger of the oxen. That was the first throne of this King. There in a stable, without man or maid, lay the Creator of all the world. And there was the maid of fifteen years bringing forth her first-born without water, fire, light, or pan, a sight for tears! . . .

Think, women, there was no one there to bathe the Baby. No warm water, nor even cold. No fire, no light. The mother was herself midwife and the maid. The cold manger was the bed and the bathtub. Who showed the poor girl what to do? She had never had a baby before. . . . Do not make of Mary a stone. It must have gone straight to her heart that she was so abandoned. She was flesh and blood, . . . not stone. For the higher people are in the favor of God, the more tender are they. . . .

I would not have you contemplate the deity of Christ, the majesty of Christ, but rather his flesh. Look upon the Baby Jesus. . . . See how God invites you. . . . He places before you a Babe in whom you may take refuge. . . . Here is the Child in whom is salvation. To me there is no greater consolation given to mankind than this, that Christ became man, a child, a babe, playing in the lap and at the breasts of his most gracious mother. . . . Now is overcome the power of sin, death, hell, conscience, and guilt, if you come to this gurgling Babe and believe that he is come, not to judge you, but to save.

Sentimental renditions of the nativity of Jesus have been a staple for a long time, to the point that Jesus's birth in a stable is made to seem charming and picturesque. There is a basic problem with that picture, namely, it is untrue. Jesus's birth was not charming. It was accompanied by deprivation and terror. Martin Luther's thoughts about the birth of Jesus are a rescue effort designed to spare us from shallow thinking about what actually happened on the night Jesus was born.

Luther was a master of the human faculty that today we call the imagination. This shows itself in two ways. First, the imagination is our capacity to identify with people and events beyond ourselves. English Romantic poet Percy Shelley described the imagination as "a going out of our own nature, and an identification of ourselves with . . . [a] thought, action, or person not our own." In the same passage, Shelley spoke of putting ourself "in the place of another" by an exercise of our imagination. This is exactly what Luther does in this meditation. Where have we ever relived the details of Jesus's birth as vividly as Luther leads us to experience them?

Secondly, the imagination contains the word *image* within it. The imagination demands an image. In literary terms, Luther's imagination is realistic, and literary realism includes the portrayal of the unidealized and unwelcome aspects of human experience. The power of Luther's recreation of the night of Jesus's birth resides in his ability to present the details as they really happened. The pathos and terror of the events register with us, and the devotional effect is that we grieve for the suffering of the characters and are moved to admire Mary and love Jesus even more.

The actual details of the nativity are inherently metaphoric and parabolic, and Luther is sensitive to this too. So in the last paragraph he expounds on the implications of the helpless humanity of the infant Jesus. A human Jesus is an approachable Jesus. Luther's final sentence is nothing less than a latent altar call to come to a *gurgling Babe* for salvation.

There is also a theological aspect to Luther's literary imagining of the night of the nativity. The theology that undergirds Luther's meditation is the humanity of Christ. In an oft-quoted sentence, Luther claims that he *would not have you contemplate the deity of Christ . . . but rather his flesh.* Jesus was both God and man. To neglect either is to distort the truth about Jesus. Bible-believing Christians can readily privilege Christ's divinity over his humanity.[20]

The edification that we can carry away from Luther's meditation is to allow the pity of the physical details of the birth of Jesus to register in our minds, and then to make sure that we understand what those details imply at metaphoric and spiritual levels.

———

Luther's imagination works its meditative magic on the following simple foundation from Luke 2:6–7:

> And while they were there, the time came for her to give birth. And she gave birth to her firstborn son and wrapped him in swaddling cloths and laid him in a manger, because there was no place for them in the inn.

PART 3

CHRISTMAS POEMS

There is no scarcity of Christmas poems, nor anthologies of them. But there *is* a scarcity of Christmas poems of sufficient quality and depth to make a significant impact on us. The majority of Christmas poems belong to the "bits and pieces" variety—brief and fleeting observations about a tiny aspect of the nativity or incarnation. The need for the entries in this anthology to yield a five-hundred-word analysis served as a sieve in which the inferior candidates fell through and the really good Christmas poems—the classic ones—remained.

The first thing that characterizes the poems in this section is that they are substantial. They cover a significant amount of meditative territory. The poets do not remain on the descriptive or observational level but move to an interpretive and analytic level. They do, indeed, make their subject come alive in our imaginations so vividly that we can relive it, but the impulse is continually to extract spiritual significance and universal relevance beyond the literal details of what happened at the first Christmas. The result is that the poems in this section do not carry all of their meaning on the surface. Accordingly, the explications that accompany the texts in this section are even more necessary to understanding the texts than in the hymn and prose sections.

Four aspects of a poem require our attention, and these will govern the explications that accompany the poems. First, a poem has a unifying topic, and within that, it makes a specific interpretive comment known as a *theme*. Second, poems are carefully organized, either by separate stanzas or units within a single composition (as in a fourteen-line sonnet). Each stanza or unit is a variation on the central theme. These variations need to be identified, and also related to the overriding superstructure. The technical term for this is *theme-and-variation*, or whole-part relationship. Third, the actual words, images, and figures of speech that embody the meanings are the poetic texture, balancing the organization or structure. The items making up the poetic texture need to have their meanings unpacked. Finally, there is an element of artistry and craftsmanship that can be noted and valued. A poem, said American poet Robert Frost, is a performance in words.

Poetry is a more concentrated form of discourse than prose. It requires more from us by way of attentiveness and close reading. This should not be regarded as a deterrent but as an invitation.

21

The Magnificat

THE VIRGIN MARY

My soul magnifies the Lord,
  and my spirit rejoices in God my Savior,
for he has looked on the humble estate of his servant.
    For behold, from now on all generations will
        call me blessed;
for he who is mighty has done great things for me,
    and holy is his name.
And his mercy is for those who fear him
    from generation to generation.
He has shown strength with his arm;
    he has scattered the proud in the thoughts of
        their hearts;
he has brought down the mighty from their thrones
    and exalted those of humble estate;
he has filled the hungry with good things,
    and the rich he has sent away empty.
He has helped his servant Israel,
    in remembrance of his mercy,
as he spoke to our fathers,
    to Abraham and to his offspring forever.
        (Luke 1:46–55)

There is a good reason to begin the section of Christmas poems with this surprise entry. The reason is that the first Christmas poems come to us from the Bible. The Gospel of Luke gives us four Christmas poems by Mary, Zechariah, the angels, and Simeon. The prologue to John's Gospel (1:1–18) is also a Christmas poem, and many of the Old Testament Messianic prophecies can be assimilated as Christmas poems.

We should start our analysis of Mary's song at the personal level of Mary herself. This is a lyric poem, and the starting point for assimilating a lyric poem is to understand that the poet speaks in a first-person ("I" and "me") format. At this level, a lyric poem is an utterance that is overheard. So as we read, we are taken inside Mary's mind and emotions. It is appropriate for us to get to know Mary as closely as possible. She was both the mother of our Savior and a godly woman who can teach us proper motions of the soul.

The original context of Mary's effusion of praise was her visit to her cousin Elizabeth. The ingredients that converged in the event were fifteen-year-old Mary with her unborn child, Elizabeth with her unborn child, and a remote hillside town. After Elizabeth blessed and praised Mary, Mary responded with the poem known to posterity as the Magnificat, named after the verb in the opening line in its Latin version. When we look at the poem as an expression of Mary's feelings of the moment, several strands are interwoven. Mary is joyful, and also surprised that a girl of poor social standing would have been selected to bear the promised Messiah. She also feels vindicated as a representative of the lowly, as over against the high and mighty, and she is aware of her honored place in the future of the world.

But Mary's feelings about her personal situation dominate only the first six lines. Her thoughts quickly telescope outward. The universe that she imagines is a triangle, the points of which are God, the needy humble (with Mary as a representative), and the oppressive powerful. These three intersect with each other within our imagined triangle.

Another way in which Mary's thoughts explode outward from her personal situation of the moment is that they encompass the past (at the end of the poem), the present, and the future. The promises of the past are the foundation for Mary's thinking about the present. But not only about the present: the present is viewed as the beginning of a revolution in human history. Mary's song announces a reversal of values in which God raises the poor and needy and puts down the privileged. This is the heart of the gospel: salvation is for those who see their need of it. Jesus himself was to say that "those who are well have no need of a physician, but those who are sick. I have not come to call the righteous but sinners to repentance" (Luke 5:31–32).[21]

As we meditate on Mary's song, we can see more and more of what is encompassed in the incarnation of Jesus, and we should heed the strong warning about thinking ourselves self-sufficient before God.

As Mary composed her thoughts, the song of Hannah recorded in 1 Samuel 2:1–10 was likely sounding in the echo chamber of her memory. That whole poem is a parallel to the Magnificat, starting with Hannah's opening declaration, "My heart exults in the LORD, . . . because I rejoice in your salvation" (v. 1). This is the true Christmas spirit.

22

A Hymn on the Nativity
of My Savior

BEN JONSON (1572–1637)

I sing the birth was born tonight,
The Author both of life and light;
The angels so did sound it,
And like the ravished shepherds said,
Who saw the light, and were afraid,
Yet searched, and true they found it.

The Son of God, the eternal King,
That did us all salvation bring,
And freed the soul from danger;
He whom the whole world could not take,
The Word, which heaven and earth did make,
Was now laid in a manger.

The Father's wisdom willed it so,
The Son's obedience knew no "No,"
Both wills were in one stature;
And as that wisdom had decreed,
The Word was now made Flesh indeed,
And took on Him our nature.

What comfort by Him do we win?
Who made Himself the Prince of sin,
To make us heirs of glory?
To see this Babe, all innocence,
A Martyr born in our defense:
Can man forget this story?

Notes on selected words. *Hymn*: poem. *Sing*: write about. *The birth was born tonight*: there is an implied ellipsis; if we supply the missing words, the statement reads "the birth *of the one that* was born tonight." *Sound it*: report it. *Like*: in the same way. *Ravished*: overcome with emotion. *Could not take*: could not contain. *Knew no "No"*: would not say "no"; in our common idiom, "did not know how to say 'no.'" *Both wills*: the will of the Father and the will of the Son. *Were in one stature*: were in unity or agreement.

Ben Jonson (1572–1637) was a contemporary of William Shakespeare in the era known as the Renaissance, which was also the age of the Reformation. This era produced the greatest quantity of Christian devotional poetry in the history of English literature, and Jonson's Christmas poem is a typical specimen.

On a first reading, the poem wins us with its apparent simplicity. The title forthrightly announces that the poem belongs to one of the most widely cultivated religious genres of Jonson's day known as the nativity poem. This is reassuring in itself, but it is intensified by the intimate epithet that Jonson uses for Jesus, namely, *My Savior*. The opening stanza too is simple. It enacts a poetic ritual known as composing the scene, in which the poet and readers imagine themselves present at the event on which the poet has chosen to meditate. Into his imagined scene Jonson imports two of the most familiar agents of the nativity—the angels and the shepherds.

After this simple opening, the poem becomes more complex. Stanzas 2–3 move from a narrative mode to an analytic or contemplative mode. The subject likewise shifts from the nativity (the birth of Jesus) to the incarnation (the theological reality of God becoming human). Stanza 2 asserts and marvels at the fact of the incarnation, while also probing the effect of it, namely, our salvation. Stanza 3 imagines an even earlier event than the birth of Jesus—what theologians call an intra-Trinitarian council of Father and Son at which the plan for the incarnation was decided.

The final stanza is governed by a tone of astonishment and wonder. These feelings are expressed in the form of three rhetorical questions (questions whose answers are self-evident). The emphasis is on what the incarnation has achieved for us, but we are also led to contemplate at what cost our *comfort* and status as *heirs* and *defense* were won, as highlighted by two unusual epithets for Jesus—*Prince of sin* and innocent *Martyr born in our defense*.[22]

If we spend the required time to absorb all of the foregoing details, we can leave the poem with a deepened understanding of what all is encompassed in the incarnation and an awakened wonder at what we possess because of it.

The following verses contain a surprising number of the ingredients that Jonson wove into the fabric of his poem: "But when the fullness of time had come, God sent forth his Son, born of woman, born under the law, to redeem those who were under the law, so that we might receive adoption as sons" (Gal. 4:4–5).

23

In the Bleak Midwinter

CHRISTINA ROSSETTI (1830–1894)

In the bleak midwinter, frosty wind made moan,
Earth stood hard as iron, water like a stone;
Snow had fallen, snow on snow, snow on snow,
In the bleak midwinter, long ago.

Our God, Heaven cannot hold Him, nor earth sustain;
Heaven and earth shall flee away when He comes
      to reign.
In the bleak midwinter a stable place sufficed
The Lord God Almighty, Jesus Christ.

Enough for Him, whom cherubim worship night
      and day,
Breastful of milk, and a mangerful of hay;
Enough for Him, whom angels fall before,
The ox and ass and camel which adore.

Angels and archangels may have gathered there,
Cherubim and seraphim thronged the air;
But His mother only, in her maiden bliss,
Worshiped the beloved with a kiss.

What can I give Him, poor as I am?
If I were a shepherd, I would bring a lamb;
If I were a Wise Man, I would do my part;
Yet what I can I give Him: give my heart.

This poem comes from the pen of a distinguished Victorian poet, Christina Rossetti (1830–1894). It requires our best analytic powers, partly because it is a poem of surprises and riddles.

The first surprise comes in the opening stanza, with its description of a frozen winter landscape. This atmospheric description is mood poetry at its best, but how does the evocation of cold and snow fit into a meditation on the birth of Jesus? One answer is that in the English-speaking world, Christmas is associated with snow and winter, as our Christmas cards abundantly confirm. "In the Bleak Midwinter" accepts this convention of a white Christmas, and so should we. Whereas the rest of this poem will situate us at the birth of Jesus in Bethlehem, the opening stanza places us in our own familiar world, perhaps evoking memories of our own Christmases reaching back to childhood.

Additionally, poetry often gains its effects by suggestion and symbolism. Many poets have used the cold winter season of Christmas to symbolize (a) the harshness of the physical surroundings into which Jesus was born, thereby highlighting the sacrificial aspect of his incarnation, and (b) the hostility of a sinful world that required the coming of a Savior. Rossetti then goes one step beyond the convention by stressing the frozen hardness of the landscape, thereby evoking a universe of death requiring something to bring it to life.

The middle three stanzas also have a riddling quality that requires us to figure out what is going on. The governing principle in each of these stanzas is that of contrast. On one side we are alerted to the fact that God is so infinite that neither the heavens nor earth can contain him, either now or when Christ returns (stanza 2). Similarly, Christ is so exalted that angels worship him and were present in glory at his nativity (stanzas 3–4). But all this grandeur is placed before us as a foil or contrast to the humble side of the nativity of Jesus. This humble dimension is the actual subject of the poem, and it is sprung on us as a surprise, as we are led to see that the most common and humble experiences *sufficed* and were *enough* for the infinite God of the universe—commonplaces like a stable, a mother's milk, animals in a barn, and the kiss of a mother on her infant.

To take stock, then, we have been situated in our imaginations in our own familiar Christmas world (stanza 1) and at the nativity (stanzas 2–4), and we have been led to see the humble aspect of Christ's birth in contrast to the majesty that deity possesses. The concluding stanza is devoted to personal application, as the note of humility reaches its climax. This stanza is structured as a problem and its solution. The question that is raised is what we can bring to the newborn Christ as an adequate gift. The speaker (and we with her) self-identifies as too poor to be able to afford an expensive gift. The answer to the question of what constitutes an adequate gift is that our heart—our self—is what we each need to give. The poem thus adheres to the time-honored literary convention of the surprise ending, as we are led to suddenly see that we do not need to search for an impressive gift; we ourself are the best gift.[23]

The primary lesson that this poem teaches is the lesson of humility, as modeled in the nativity of Jesus. A mother's milk and a manger with hay are said to suffice for the King of kings. The acts that matter most are a mother's kiss and the gift of a poor person's heart.

With this lesson in humility ringing in our ears, we think naturally of Philippians 2:8: "And being found in human form, he humbled himself by becoming obedient to the point of death, even death on a cross."

24

The Consecration of the Common Way

EDWIN MARKHAM (1852–1940)

The hills that had been lone and lean
Were pricking with a tender green,
And flocks were whitening over them
From all the folds of Bethlehem.

The King of Heaven had come our way,
And in a lowly stable lay;
He had descended from the sky
In answer to the world's long cry—
Descended in a lyric burst
Of high archangels, going first
Unto the lowest and the least,
To humble bird and weary beast,
His palace was a wayside shed,
A battered manger was his bed;
An ox and ass with breathings deep
Made warm the chamber of his sleep.

Three sparrows with a friendly sound
Were pricking barley from the ground;
An early sunbeam, long and thin,
Slanted across the dark within,
And brightened in its silver fall
A cart-wheel leaning to the wall.
An ox-yoke hung upon a hook;
A worn plow with a clumsy crook
Was lying idly by the wheel.
And everywhere there was the feel
Of that sweet peace that labor brings—
The peace that dwells with homely things.

Now have the homely things been made
Sacred, and a glory on them laid,
For He whose shelter was a stall,
The King, was born among them all.
He came to handle saw and plane,
To use and follow the profane;
Now is the holy not afar
In temples lighted by a star,
But where the loves and labors are,
Now that the King has gone this way,
Great are the things of every day!

The nativity story in Luke is laden with secondary themes and over-tones that radiate out from the spiritual center. That center is the story of redemption: Jesus was born in order to save his people from their sin. But secondary meanings are also an important part of the Christmas story.

Many who have written devotionally on the birth of Jesus have seen spiritual significance in the humble circumstances of the birth, often seeing in it an implied rebuke of pomp and wealth. For example, Martin Luther said in a Christmas sermon,

Behold how very ordinary and common things on earth seem to us, and yet how high they are regarded in heaven. . . . [In Christ's birth] God lets the large houses and costly apartments remain empty. . . . See how God shows that he utterly disregards what the world desires.

In a similar vein, John Calvin observed that the message of Christ's birth was announced first to common "unlearned men and poor shepherds," not "to the great ones of this world, nor to the wise, nor to the rich, nor to nobles." This is the spirit in which we must assimilate Edwin Markham's (1852–1940) poem.

One reason Markham's poem is such a well-known statement of the truth we are considering is that the title and last line of the poem encapsulate the principle in its pure form. The principle is *the common way* and *the things of every day*. What exactly does the nativity teach about ordinary experience and common things? That they have been consecrated or made sacred by Christ's immersion in them.

Whereas many poems assert their themes in the opening line, Markham reversed that order and built his entire poem around the final line. The effect of this summary line is to cast a retrospective look over everything that has preceded, prompting us to see how every detail has been carefully chosen and positioned to build up to the conclusion.

The brief opening stanza places us in our imagination at the physical place of the nativity. The second stanza then introduces action into that scene in the form of the coming of the *King of Heaven* to a *lowly stable*. Because the main thrust of the poem is to elevate the common life, Markham expands the birth scene with far more images of everyday life than the nativity story in Luke's Gospel does. Images of the common life totally occupy the third stanza, with only a hint of the nativity that occurred in the midst of these objects and activities.

Up to this point, we have cause to wonder how all of this descriptive detail fits into a Christmas poem. The final stanza comes to our rescue by giving us a complete interpretation of what has been described in the first three stanzas: the common way has been made sacred by Christ's birth and earthly life. In keeping with the elevation of the common, the poem is written in the simple verse form of couplets (pairs of lines that end with the same rhyming sound, as in *lean* and *green*).[24]

The devotional lesson that we can carry away from the poem is that Jesus in his birth gives us a model for embracing the common life as something that God values supremely and that is therefore sacred. We can ponder how the mundane circumstances of Christ's birth might affect our attitudes toward the commonplace duties and experiences of our daily routines.

A parallel to Markham's poem is Zechariah 14:20, a memorable statement of the sanctity of common things:

> On that day there shall be inscribed on the bells of the horses, "Holy to the LORD." And the pots in the house of the LORD shall be as the bowls before the altar.

25

A Christmas Carol

G. K. CHESTERTON (1874–1936)

The Christ-child lay on Mary's lap,
His hair was like a light.
(O weary, weary were the world,
But here is all aright.)

The Christ-child lay on Mary's breast
His hair was like a star.
(O stern and cunning are the kings,
But here the true hearts are.)

The Christ-child lay on Mary's heart,
His hair was like a fire.
(O weary, weary is the world,
But here the world's desire.)

The Christ-child stood on Mary's knee,
His hair was like a crown,
And all the flowers looked up at Him,
And all the stars looked down.

G. K. Chesterton (1874–1936) was such an enthusiast for the English and American institution of Christmas that over a span of thirty years he published at least five articles on Christmas every year. He was particularly appreciative of the paradoxes of Christmas. He claimed, for example, that Christmas is "built upon a beautiful . . . paradox: that the birth of the homeless should be celebrated in every home." Again, "Christ Himself was a Christmas present." As Chesterton contemplated the humble shepherds of the nativity, and what Mary herself called her "low estate" (the Magnificat), he was led to pen the line "Glory to God in the lowest."

Chesterton's best known Christmas poem, printed here, fits this pattern by being a paradoxical poem. It is commonly regarded as a children's Christmas poem, so we should look at that aspect of the poem first. The situation presented is the familiar mother and child scene—the Madonna and child so famous in painting and sculpture. The opening line of each stanza keeps this domestic situation in the forefront by placing the infant Jesus successively on his mother's *lap*, *breast*, *heart*, and *knee*, thereby awakening the physical sensations of being cuddled by a mother. We should also note the ease of reading that we feel with the brief stanzas, the short lines, and the lilting rhythm. At these levels the poem is, indeed, a child's poem.

But there are other aspects of the poem that make it an adult poem as well as a child's poem. The next-to-last lines of the first three stanzas zoom outward from the safe domestic scene of infant and mother into a hostile world that is said to be *weary, weary,* and terrorized by *stern and cunning kings*. But in each case, to our relief we are immediately pulled back into a world where *all is aright*, where *true hearts are*, and where we find *the world's desire*. What adult does not know the experience of having feelings of well-being shattered by the inroads of a weary and threatening world and then returning to the safety of peaceful assurance. We cannot miss the point that the discordant note drops out of sight in the final stanza, showing that the birth of the Christ-child brought final triumph over evil.

An even bigger interpretive challenge is posed by the fantasy element in the poem. This has to do with the treatment of Jesus's hair, which in successive stanzas is compared in simile to a *light*, a *star*, a *fire*, and a *crown*. We are faced with a riddle that requires solving. Probably Chesterton intends a symbolic effect of transcendence—a way of portraying the divinity of this child. This then reaches a climax in the final stanza, with its picture of the flowers looking up and the stars looking down in an act of homage to the Christ-child who is the focal point of reality.[25]

———

Reliving this note of homage combined with the innocence of the domestic scene is how we can assimilate this poem of calm—a poem that reminds us of the sense of repose also expressed in the hymn "Silent Night" (see page 31).

———

The scene that this poem invites us to linger over is the same scene that the wise men experienced:

> And going into the house, they saw the child with Mary his mother, and they fell down and worshiped him. (Matt. 2:11)

26

A Christmas Hymn

RICHARD WILBUR (1921–2017)

And some of the Pharisees from among the multitude said unto him, Master, rebuke thy disciples. And he answered and said unto them, I tell you that, if these should hold their peace, the stones would immediately cry out. (Luke 19:39–40)

A stable-lamp is lighted
Whose glow shall wake the sky;
The stars shall bend their voices,
And every stone shall cry.
And every stone shall cry,
And straw like gold shall shine;
A barn shall harbor heaven,
A stall become a shrine.

This child through David's city
Shall ride in triumph by;
The palm shall strew its branches,
And every stone shall cry.
And every stone shall cry,
Though heavy, dull, and dumb,
And lie within the roadway
To pave His kingdom come.

Yet He shall be forsaken,
And yielded up to die;
The sky shall groan and darken,
And every stone shall cry.
And every stone shall cry
For stony hearts of men:
God's blood upon the spearhead,
God's love refused again.

But now, as at the ending,
The low is lifted high;
The stars shall bend their voices,
And every stone shall cry.
And every stone shall cry
In praises of the child
By whose descent among us
The worlds are reconciled.

———

Richard Wilbur (1921–2017) was a college professor and prolific twentieth-century poet. He even served a term as poet laureate of the United States. When receiving a lifetime award from the Conference on Christianity and Literature, he affirmed that his entire poetic corpus had been shaped by Christianity.

Because Wilbur is a modern poet, we are not surprised that "A Christmas Hymn" initially baffles us. But with the right interpretive pointers at our disposal, the complexity subsides, and we come to see that the poem is actually quite simple and accessible.

We can begin with the overall lay of the land. Stanzas 1, 2, and 4 read like a conventional Christmas poem that rejoices in the nativity of Jesus. All of the expected images are present—*stable, sky, stars, straw, child, David's city, reconciled worlds*. To make the spirit of celebration even more festive, stanza 2 intertwines the story of Christ's triumphal entry into Jerusalem with the story of the nativity. But stanza 3 inserts a contrary note of sadness into the poem by taking us in imagination to the scene of Christ's crucifixion.

What is Good Friday doing in a Christmas poem? It is there to remind us of the reason for Christ's coming to earth in a body that died. One theme of the poem can thus be summarized by the formula "without Good Friday, no Christmas," and equally, "without Christmas, no Good Friday." In mastering the poem, we need to unpack the meanings of those truths.

The epigraph from the story of the triumphal entry, combined with the fact that the line *and every stone shall cry* appears in tandem right in the middle of each stanza, requires us to determine what this means. When Jesus said that if his followers were silenced the stones would cry out, he was asserting that the world is so constituted that nothing can prevent his worthiness from being acknowledged. Applied to Christmas, we are given to understand that the world not only *should* celebrate Christ's coming but that it *does* celebrate it. In the opening line of the last stanza, the poet subtly anticipates that the world will again lift Christ high as it did at his nativity when he comes *at the ending* of human history.[26]

This poem can do two complementary things for us: it can give voice to our exalting of Christ as we relive the nativity in our imagination, and it can caution us against a shallow celebration of Christmas by reminding us of the sinfulness of the human race that crucified Christ.

"A Christmas Hymn" asks us to celebrate Christ's coming in an awareness that the fallen world rejects its Savior. The prologue to John's Gospel, itself a Christmas poem, sounds an identical note: "The true light, which gives light to everyone, was coming into the world. He was in the world, and the world was made through him, yet the world did not know him" (John 1:9–10).

97

27

No Room for Jesus

AUTHOR UNKNOWN (1600S)

Yet if his majesty our sovereign lord,
Should of his own accord
Friendly himself invite,
And say "I'll be your guest to-morrow night,"
How should we stir ourselves, call and command
All hands to work! "Let no man idle stand.

Set me fine Spanish tables in the hall,
See they be fitted all;
Let there be room to eat,
And order taken that there want no meat.
See every sconce and candlestick made bright,
That without tapers they may give a light.

Look to the presence: are the carpets spread,
The dazie o'er the head,
The cushions in the chairs,
And all the candles lighted on the stairs?
Perfume the chambers, and in any case
Let each man give attendance in his place."

Thus if the king were coming would we do,
And 'twere good reason too;
For 'tis a duteous thing
To show all honor to an earthly king,
And after all our travail and our cost,
So he be pleased, to think no labor lost.

But at the coming of the King of Heaven
All's set at six and seven:
We wallow in our sin,
Christ cannot find a chamber in the inn.
We entertain him always like a stranger,
And as at first still lodge him in the manger.

Notes on selected words. *His majesty our sovereign lord*: a stately epithet [title] for the king of England. *Sconce*: wall-mounted candlestick.
Presence: royal chamber. *Dazie*: dais or canopy, perhaps over the head
table. *Duteous*: dutiful. *Travail*: labor. *Set at six and seven*: in a state
of confusion and disarray.

———————

There are several things that make this seventeenth-century poem
unique among the entries in this anthology. It is the only text whose
author is unknown. Additionally, whereas it is common for Christmas devotionals to include an element of rebuke to Christian readers
or listeners for their sinfulness or negligence, this is the only selection that is given solely to a rebuke of the reader. In keeping with
this rhetoric of rebuke, the genre too is unique: whereas Christmas
hymns and poems are *arrival* poems that celebrate Christ's *coming*
to earth and being *received* there, this poem is a *rejection* poem in
which earth ignores Jesus.

The backdrop of this nativity poem is the detail in Luke 2 that
there was no room in the inn when the time came for Mary to deliver
the baby Jesus. Many of the literal details in the birth stories of the

Gospels are laden with symbolic overtones. For example, the humble status of Mary and Joseph and the shepherds has been seen as God's consecration of the commonplace. This poem correctly sees a universal principle in the fact that society did not find a place for Jesus on the night of his birth.

To depict this rejection of the worthy one, the poet has constructed a heightened contrast as the organizational pattern of the poem. The first four stanzas create a picture of the frenzied attentiveness that the world gives when a king or dignitary pays a visit, and then contrasts that in the last stanza to the indifference that people show to the divine King of the universe. We experience the last stanza as a supreme irony—a reversal of what should be. It is a stanza that convicts us.

The first four stanzas gain their effect by the detailed portrayal of the interior architecture and household routines in an English palace or great house. This is obviously an insider's description, and part of the pleasure of the poem comes from allowing ourselves to be whisked away in our imagination to what it was like to live in an aristocratic English house. These stanzas catch us up in the excitement of getting a great house ready for a festive celebration. As we read those stanzas, we have no way of knowing that the main point of the poem is spiritual.

The excitement of anticipation comes to a sudden halt in the final stanza. The great house is replaced by a barn and *manger*, and the king of the realm is replaced by an unknown *stranger*. This is an implied metaphor for how the fallen human race and we ourselves fail to give the precedence to Jesus that he deserves.[27]

———

The devotional force of the poem that we can carry away resides in the voice of accusation that we encounter in the final stanza; we should leave the poem with a resolve in our minds and hearts to give Christ the precedence that he should have.

———

In the middle of the Christmas poem that opens the Gospel of John, we find a parallel to the idea that constitutes the whole of this poem: Christ "came to his own, and his own people did not receive him" (John 1:11).

28

Wilt Thou Love God as He Thee?

JOHN DONNE (1572–1631)

Wilt thou love God, as he thee? Then digest,
My soul, this wholesome meditation:
How God the Spirit, by angels waited on
In heaven, doth make his Temple in thy breast.
The Father having begot a Son most blest,
And still begetting—for he ne'er begun—
Hath deigned to choose thee by adoption,
Co-heir to his glory, and Sabbath's endless rest.
And as a robbed man, which by search doth find
His stolen stuff sold, must lose or buy it again,
The Son of glory came down, and was slain,
Us whom he had made and Satan stolen, to unbind.
'Twas much, that man was made like God before,
But, that God should be made like man, much more.

Notes on selected words. *Digest*: absorb. *Wholesome*: health-promoting; beneficial. *Waited on*: served or attended to. *Breast*: heart or soul; the spiritual self. *Begetting*: a theological and Trinitarian term shrouded in mystery; Donne is playing on the terminology that Jesus is the "begotten" Son of the Father. *Deigned*: condescended.

Sabbath's endless rest: eternal life in heaven. *Before*: at the creation and forward from then. *Much*: very significant.

John Donne (1572–1631) is one of the towering poets of English literature, and also one of the most famous preachers in English ecclesiastical history. The sonnet (a fourteen-line poem) printed here is a meditative poem par excellence. Its subject is the incarnation, but that is not how the meditative topic is presented at the outset. Instead, the opening question invites us to intensify our love for God in response to his love toward us. As we keep reading, we are led to think about the incarnation of Jesus in new ways.

We should note in advance that the poet is thinking in terms of the three persons of the Trinity, each of whom receives separate attention. Additionally, we need to keep in mind that the announced theme of the meditation is how we can love God the way he loves us (line 1). First we are led to contemplate how the God of heaven resides within us through the agency of the Holy Spirit (lines 3–4).

In the next four lines (5–8), we are prompted to meditate on how the Father of heaven adopts us and makes us co-heirs with his Son. The next four-line unit (lines 9–12) is what makes the poem a Christmas poem. By means of a vivid simile involving recovering stolen property, we are led to think about the nature of Christ's coming to earth and dying to release sinful humanity from Satan.

All of the foregoing has already displayed Donne's trademark originality, but the last two lines (a rhyming couplet) have the effect of a surprise ending. Christian theology has made much of the fact that people are created in the image of God, but the incarnation is suddenly presented to us as a reversal of that common formula, as we are told that in the incarnation, God was made in the image of man.[28]

To make this poem a permanent possession, we need to ponder the individual angles of vision that unfold before us, always with a view toward doing what the opening question invites us to do, namely, love God in response to his love for us.

This poem is a mosaic of biblical allusions. Philippians 2:8 can serve as a summary of the poem's overall argument:

And being found in human form, he humbled himself by becoming obedient to the point of death, even death on a cross.

29

On the Morning of Christ's Nativity

JOHN MILTON (1608–1674)

This is the month, and this the happy morn,
Wherein the Son of Heaven's eternal King,
Of wedded maid and virgin mother born,
Our great redemption from above did bring;
For so the holy sages once did sing,
That he our deadly forfeit should release,
And with his Father work us a perpetual peace.

That glorious form, that light unsufferable,
And that far-beaming blaze of majesty,
Wherewith he wont at Heaven's high council-table
To sit the midst of Trinal Unity,
He laid aside, and, here with us to be
Forsook the courts of everlasting day,
And chose with us a darksome house of mortal clay.

Notes on selected words. *The holy sages*: the Old Testament prophets.
Forfeit: penalty; loss of a right. *Glorious form*: Christ's divine person,
exalted in heaven. *Unsufferable*: too intense to be endured by humans,
a reference to 1 Timothy 6:16, which tells us that God "dwells in

unapproachable light, whom no one has ever seen or can see." *Wont*: accustomed. *Midst*: in the middle of. *Trinal Unity*: the triune Godhead. *Darksome house of mortal clay*: physical human body.

These two stanzas are the opening of John Milton's (1608–1674) exalted ode composed early on Christmas morning while Milton was home during vacation from Cambridge University. They can be read and enjoyed as a freestanding reflection on the meaning of Christ's incarnation.

The opening line is a stroke of genius, and it alerts us that the best possible time to read and reread Milton's poem is on Christmas morning. *This is the month, and this the happy morn*: which December 25 is in view? The morning when Christ was born? Christmas day on 1629, when Milton composed the poem before daybreak? Or any Christmas on which we read the poem? Milton opened the way for us to see all three meanings.

The subject of Milton's celebration on Christmas day is not the nativity but the incarnation—not the event of Christ's birth but its theological meaning. Thus the key words in the opening stanza are theological in nature—*redemption* and salvation, *release* and *perpetual peace*.

The second stanza moves from reflection on how Christ's incarnation brought us redemption from the penalty of sin to a brief narrative of how Jesus came down from heaven to earth. Until we reach the last line, the images evoke a sense of transcendent glory beyond the earthly. Then the last line springs a sudden contrast on us with its picture of *a darksome house of mortal clay*. We are shocked into seeing the tremendous sacrifice that the incarnation represents.

In keeping with the exaltation of the subject matter, Milton writes in the high style. The sentences are long and suspended, meaning that we need to keep reading and reading before we reach the main sentence element (line 4 in the first stanza and line 5 in the second). Epithets (exalted titles) abound, such as *the Son of Heaven's eternal King* as a title for Christ, *the holy sages* for the Old Testament prophets, and *the courts of everlasting day* for heaven.[29]

When we read these stanzas on Christmas morning (either literally or in our imagination), we can allow Milton to be our guide to (a) pondering how the incarnation is the instrument of our redemption, and (b) being thankful for the Son's willingness to come down from heaven to earth.

The subjects of the respective stanzas in Milton's poem are redemption (stanza 1) and divine condescension, or coming down to humanity (stanza 2). The Christ hymn in Philippians 2 presents these same two themes, but in reverse order:

> Who, though he was in the form of God, did not count equality with God a thing to be grasped, but emptied himself, by taking the form of a servant, being born in the likeness of men. And being found in human form, he humbled himself by becoming obedient to the point of death, even death on a cross. (vv. 6–8)

30

Journey of the Magi

T. S. ELIOT (1888–1965)

"A cold coming we had of it,
Just the worst time of the year
For a journey, and such a long journey:
The ways deep and the weather sharp,
The very dead of winter."
And the camels galled, sorefooted, refractory,
Lying down in the melting snow.
There were times we regretted
The summer palaces on slopes, the terraces,
And the silken girls bringing sherbet.
Then the camel men cursing and grumbling
and running away, and wanting their liquor and
        women,
And the night-fires going out, and the lack of
        shelters,
And the cities hostile and the towns unfriendly
And the villages dirty and charging high prices:
A hard time we had of it.
At the end we preferred to travel all night,
Sleeping in snatches,
With the voices singing in our ears, saying
That this was all folly.

Then at dawn we came down to a temperate valley,
Wet, below the snow line, smelling of vegetation;
With a running stream and a water-mill beating the
    darkness,
And three trees on the low sky,
And an old white horse galloped away in the
    meadow.
Then we came to a tavern with vine-leaves over the
    lintel,
Six hands at an open door dicing for pieces of silver,
And feet kicking the empty wine-skins.
But there was no information, and so we continued
And arriving at evening, not a moment too soon
Finding the place; it was (you might say) satisfactory.

All this was a long time ago, I remember,
And I would do it again, but set down
This set down
This: were we led all that way for
Birth or Death? There was a Birth, certainly;
We had evidence and no doubt. I had seen birth
    and death,
But had thought they were different; this Birth was
Hard and bitter agony for us, like Death, our death.
We returned to our places, these Kingdoms,
But no longer at ease here, in the old dispensation,
With an alien people clutching their gods.
I should be glad of another death.

Notes on selected words. *The magi*: the wise men who traveled to visit the infant Jesus. *Quotation marks surrounding the first five lines*: these lines are a nearly verbatim quotation from a Christmas sermon by the Renaissance Anglican preacher Lancelot Andrewes (see page 45). *Galled*: in pain. *Refractory*: stubborn or unmanageable. *Dispensation*: social order with its institutions, practices, and values.

This poem was part of a series of "Christmas cards" authored by contemporary poets and published annually in the late 1920s by the publishing house for which T. S. Eliot worked as an editor. Whereas conventional Christmas cards treat the journey of the wise men sentimentally, Eliot's poem presents a consistent bleakness that leads us to see the sacrificial nature of Christ's coming to earth. This was the first poem in which Eliot expressed his Christian faith after publicly announcing his conversion, perhaps explaining how he came to write a poem whose ending places it in the genre of conversion poem.

In form, this poem is a dramatic monologue, meaning that the speaker addresses an implied listener in a specific situation that we infer. The speaker is one of the wise men in his old age. He is speaking to someone who is taking notes. The action that unfolds is the wise man's reminiscence of his journey and its effect in his life. First the speaker recreates the physical details of the journey. Then he analyzes the event and extracts its spiritual meaning. The speaker's words thus combine narration and reflection.

Each stanza is distinctively different from the others. The first stanza uses the techniques of realism to narrate the physical and psychological hardships of the journey. The second stanza employs conventional Christian symbolism and biblical allusions to establish the sacrificial nature of incarnation. In the third stanza, the wise man interprets his experience. If we read these lines carefully, we see that the speaker is now a Christian believer for whom the *Death* (capitalized) of Christ is *our death* (a substitutionary death). Life in an *alien* culture is so difficult that the speaker would be *glad of another death*. The meaning of this line is that the speaker longs for physical death as the gate to eternal life in heaven.

We expect a modern poem to avoid sentimentality, and this one does. The journey is described as a physical horror. The images and allusions in the second stanza evoke the fallen nature of the world that Christ came to save, and references to *three trees* (crosses) silhouetted against the sky and a *lintel* take us in imagination to the crucifixion and the Passover. In the final stanza, the speaker's experience of isolation as a believer in a hostile society is every believer's experience.[30]

Eliot's poem can lead us to meditate on the sacrificial dimension of the life and death of the incarnate Christ and also on the cost of being a Christian in an alien society.

Eliot's poem emphasizes the sacrificial purpose of Christ's incarnation and the way in which people who place their faith in Jesus become aliens in their surrounding culture. The Epistle of 1 Peter is built around that same twofold premise, as epitomized in the following passage:

> Conduct yourselves with fear throughout the time of your exile, knowing that you were ransomed . . . with the precious blood of Christ, . . . [who] was made manifest in the last times for the sake of you who through him are believers in God. (1 Pet. 1:17–21)

Acknowledgments

Explications of the ten Christmas hymns (pages 3–33) incorporate material taken from *40 Favorite Hymns of the Christian Year* by Leland Ryken. ISBN 978-1-62995-793-7; used with permission from P&R Publishing Co., www.prpbooks.com.

For the excerpt from John Calvin on pages 37–38: *Songs of the Nativity*, translated and edited by Robert White (Edinburgh: Banner of Truth, 2008), 19–31. Reprinted by permission.

For the excerpt from Augustine on pages 49–50: Excerpts from *St. Augustine Sermons for Christmas and Epiphany (ACW)*, translated and annotated by Thomas Lawler Comerford, Copyright © 1952 by Rev. Johannes Questen and Rev. Joseph C. Plumpe, Published by Newman Press, an imprint of Paulist Press, Inc., New York/Mahwah, NJ. Reprinted by permission of Paulist Press, Inc. www.paulistpress.com.

For the excerpt from Martin Luther on page pages 73–74: *The Martin Luther Christmas Book*, translated and edited by Roland Bainton (Philadelphia: Westminster Press, 1948), 35–40; reprinted by permission of Westminster John Knox Press.

"A Christmas Hymn" by Richard Wilbur (on pages 95–96) was reprinted from *Collected Poems 1943–2004*. Copyright © 2004 by Richard Wilbur. Reprinted by permission of Mariner Books, an imprint of HarperCollins Publishers LLC.

"Journey of the Magi" by T. S. Eliot (on pages 108–9) was reprinted from *Collected Poems 1909–1962* by T. S. Eliot. Copyright © 1936 by Houghton Mifflin Harcourt Publishing Company, renewed 1964 by Thomas Stearns Eliot. Reprinted by permission of Mariner Books, an imprint of HarperCollins Publishers LLC.

Notes

All of the texts in this anthology, by virtue of being classic texts, are surrounded by a body of common knowledge. To offer a source for this shared information would be misleading and inaccurate because the data appears in many places. I have therefore not provided documentation for this material. Unless otherwise noted and acknowledged, all texts are in the public domain. I have included a note for every entry, containing information about publication and sources as I thought appropriate and interesting to my readers.

1. "Joy to the World" was first published in 1719 in Isaac Watts's collection *The Psalms of David: Imitated in the Language of the New Testament, and Applied to the Christian State. . . .* Watts himself shared that he had based the poem on Psalms 98 and 96:11–12, as well as Genesis 3:17–18. As hinted in the subtitle of the hymnbook in which this poem was published, Watts gave these Old Testament texts a Christological application.
2. "Angels from the Realms of Glory" was first printed as a poem in the newspaper that the author, James Montgomery, owned in Sheffield, Ireland, on December 24, 1816. The poem became a hymn when it was paired with music and sung in a Moravian Church in England on Christmas Day in 1821. It became well known when it was published in *The Christian Psalmist* in 1825.
3. "Come, Thou Long-Expected Jesus" was first printed in 1745 in a small volume of eighteen hymns titled *Hymns for the Nativity of Our Lord* (see entry for this hymn: Chris Fenner "Come, Thou Long-Expected Jesus," Hymnology Archive, August 27, 2020, https://www.hymnologyarchive.com). The link between the hymn and Haggai 2:7 appears in numerous internet and print sources,

including Ace Collins, *More Stories behind the Best-Loved Songs of Christmas* (Grand Rapids, MI: Zondervan, 2006), 100. The poetic form of the poem most obviously calls for a four-quatrain arrangement, and some hymnbooks use music that calls for this format; the music in other hymnbooks requires packaging as two eight-line stanzas.

4. "Brightest and Best of the Sons of the Morning" was written in 1811 and published in 1827 in a volume of hymns compiled by Reginald Heber's widow. Reginald Heber was a high-church Anglican clergyman committed to the liturgical calendar. In that calendar, the journey of the wise men is featured on the Sunday of Epiphany. The word *epiphany* means "revelation," inasmuch as Christ was revealed to Gentiles when the star led the wise men to Bethlehem. In liturgical circles, this hymn is a standard epiphany hymn. A degree of controversy has swirled around Heber's opening line. Why did he call the star a son of the morning? Possibly he wanted "two for the price of one." When we first read or sing the opening line, we do not yet know that it refers to the eastern star of the wise men; our natural impulse is to think it refers to Christ. Furthermore, given the imprecision that characterizes the singing of hymns as opposed to reading and analyzing them, it is probable that most people sing the line as an exalted epithet for Christ. There is nothing wrong with this: Jesus is both the Son and "the bright morning star" (Rev. 22:16), so it is endearing to think of him as "brightest and best of the sons of the morning."

5. "It Came upon the Midnight Clear" was written for a Sunday school class and first published as a poem in 1849 in a Boston weekly called *The Christian Register*. It was paired with music the next year.

6. "Once in Royal David's City" was first published in a collection of poems for children in 1848. It became a Christmas carol the next year when a composer wrote music specifically for it. The original poem was comprised of six stanzas. The two stanzas in the middle were didactic stanzas about Christ as the pattern of an obedient child, and an exhortation to children to be obedient as Christ was. I have not included these two stanzas. They are a distraction from the main identity of the poem, which is about the nativity and its purpose of bringing many sons and daughters to glory.

7. "As with Gladness Men of Old" was written on Epiphany Day, January 6, 1859, when William Chatterton Dix was prevented by illness from attending the Epiphany church service in his hometown of Bristol, England. He included the poem (not yet set to music) in a self-printed volume titled *Hymns of Love and Joy*, and it was also printed in a church hymnal of a local church in his hometown. Music was added when the Anglican *Hymns Ancient and Modern* included the poem in their 1861 hymnal.

8. "Hark! The Herald Angels Sing" was published almost immediately after it was composed in a hymnbook titled *Hymns and Sacred Poems* (1739), a volume for which John and Charles Wesley served as the moving spirits. George Whitefield introduced his tweaks for a 1753 hymnbook that he edited, titled *A Collection of Hymns for Social Worship*.

9. "O Little Town of Bethlehem" was written for the children in Phillips Brooks's church in December of 1865. The music was composed by the church's music director, who recalled that the hymn was then printed on leaflets and sold in center city Philadelphia. In 1870, E. P. Dutton (New York) published the hymn in a hymnbook. (I have gleaned this information from Chris Fenner, "O Little Town of Bethlehem," Hymnology Archive, December 2, 2019, https://www.hymnologyarchive.com.)

10. "Silent Night" was composed in 1816 by a young German Catholic priest. It was first sung on Christmas Eve in 1818, and then gained currency through a traveling singing group. It was first published in 1833. *Time* magazine reached its conclusion that this is "the most popular Christmas song ever" on the basis of copyright records; the article that reported the finding is as follows: Chris Wilson, "This Is the Most Popular Christmas Song Ever," *Time*, Dec. 2, 2014, https://time.com.

11. John Calvin's thoughts on Mary as our example have been taken from a volume of his Christmas sermons titled *Songs of the Nativity*, trans. and ed. Robert White (Edinburgh: Banner of Truth, 2008), 19–31. Permission to reprint the material is hereby gratefully acknowledged.

12. Bernard of Clairvaux's praise of Bethlehem was reprinted from *Sermons of St. Bernard on Advent and Christmas* (London: R and T Washbourne, 1909), 75–80. Martin Luther's outburst against Bethlehem is well storied and appears in multiple online and print

sources, including Roland Bainton, *The Martin Luther Christmas Book* (Philadelphia, PA: Westminster Press, 1948), 35.

13. The passage from Lancelot Andrewes was taken from his book *Seventeen Sermons on the Nativity* (London: Griffith, Farran, Okeden, and Welsh, 1887), 252–59.

14. The paradoxes of the incarnation stated by Augustine were gleaned from a book of Augustine's *Sermons for Christmas and Epiphany*, trans. Thomas Comerford Lawler (Westminster, MD: The Newman Press, 1952), 98–99, 104–6, 115. Reprinted by the gracious permission of Paulist Press. A succinct summary of the relation of John's prologue to the Hymn to Zeus and of Augustine's encounter with John's statement about the Word becoming flesh is available on a single page in William M. Ramsey, *The Westminster Guide to the Books of the Bible* (Louisville, KY: Westminster John Knox Press, 1994), 530.

15. The author of the 1918 bidding prayer was Eric Milner-White, dean of the chapel at King's College, Cambridge. The text of the bidding prayer used in this anthology was taken from a public domain website.

16. The excerpt from Charles Spurgeon's sermon "The Great Birthday" was taken from *Metropolitan Tabernacle Pulpit Volume 22* (London: Passmore and Alabaster, 1876). The sermon is available on multiple public domain websites.

17. The Nicene Creed as printed in this anthology is a lightly modernized version of the text found in the 1892 Book of Common Prayer, available from multiple internet and print sources.

18. The selection from Athanasius was pieced together from his book *On the Incarnation of the Word of God*, trans. T. Herbert Bindley (London: The Religious Tract Society, 1905). The text has been lightly modernized.

19. All but the last paragraph of the meditation by Jonathan Edwards was excerpted from his sermon "The Excellency of Christ," preached in 1736, published in 1738, and widely available in public domain web and print sources. The final paragraph comes from Edwards's treatise *A History of Redemption*, as printed in *The Works of President Edwards* (New York: Robert Carter and Brothers, 1861), 1:398–99.

20. The selection from Martin Luther is reprinted from *The Martin Luther Christmas Book*, translated and edited by Roland Bainton

(Philadelphia, PA: Westminster Press, 1948), 35–40; reprinted by permission of Westminster John Knox Press. The quotations from Shelley are from his essay *A Defence of Poetry*.

21. Mary's "Magnificat" is recorded in the Gospel of Luke (1:46–55).

22. Ben Jonson's "A Hymn on the Nativity of My Savior" was first published in Jonson's book titled *Underwoods* in 1640.

23. Christina Rossetti's "In the Bleak Midwinter" was first published under the title "A Christmas Carol" in the January 1872 issue of *Scribner's Monthly*. It was first published in book form in Rossetti's volume *Goblin Market, The Prince's Progress and Other Poems* (London: Macmillan, 1875).

24. Edwin Markham's poem "The Consecration of the Common Way" was reprinted from the book where it was originally published: *The Shoes of Happiness and Other Poems* (Garden City, NY: Doubleday, Page and Co., 1915), 176–77. The quotation from Martin Luther comes from his 1521 sermon "The Story of the Birth of Jesus and the Angels' Song," and the the quotation from Calvin comes from his "Sermon on the Nativity of Jesus Christ;" both were accessed from public domain websites.

25. "A Christmas Carol," by G. K. Chesterton, was reprinted from the original published version as it appeared in Chesterton's book *The Wild Knight and Other Poems* (London: Grant Richards, 1900). The brief quotations from Chesterton in my commentary were gleaned from assorted websites and are readily available from multiple web and print sources.

26. "A Christmas Hymn" by Richard Wilbur was published in *Collected Poems 1943–2004*. Copyright © 2004 by Richard Wilbur. Reprinted by permission of Mariner Books, an imprint of HarperCollins Publishers LLC. Richard Wilbur's views on the relation of his life and poetry to Christianity can be found in a long interview: "Richard Wilbur," *Christianity & Literature* 41, no. 4 (Summer 1992), 520–21, https://www.christianityandliterature.com.

27. "No Room for Jesus" was discovered in a seventeenth-century manuscript in the library of Christ Church, a college of Oxford University. The manuscript does not contain an author's name. The person who discovered the poem theorized that the seventeenth-century devotional poet Henry Vaughan (1621–1695) may have been the author; however, today it is often ascribed to the composer Thomas Ford (1580–1648). Most anthologies that include

this poem use the opening line as the title, an awkward title to be sure (the more so because, as the person who discovered the manuscript and first published the poem theorized, the opening is so abrupt as to suggest that some opening lines have been lost). A few anthologies title the poem "The Stranger." When including it in this anthology, I gave it a title that names what the poem is actually about.

28. John Donne's "Wilt Thou Love God as He Thee?" is part of a posthumous collection of *Holy Sonnets*, first published in 1633.

29. "On the Morning of Christ's Nativity" was first published in *Poems of Mr. John Milton* (London: Thomas Dring, 1645).

30. T. S. Eliot's "Journey of the Magi" was reprinted from *Collected Poems 1909–1962* by T. S. Eliot. Copyright © 1936 by Houghton Mifflin Harcourt Publishing Company, renewed 1964 by Thomas Stearns Eliot. Reprinted by permission of Mariner Books, an imprint of HarperCollins Publishers LLC.

Person Index

Scripture Index

Scripture Index